WHEN

IN

DOUBT,

STOP

THE

BOUT

WHEN
IN
DOUBT,
A REVOLUTIONARY APPROACH
STOP
THE
BOUT
TO BOXING SAFETY AND REFORM

Mike Silver

HAMILCAR
PUBLICATIONS
Boston

Publisher's Cataloging-in-Publication Data

Names: Silver, Mike, author.
Title: When in doubt , stop the bout : a revolutionary approach to boxing
  safety and reform / Mike Silver.
Description: Includes bibliographical references. | Boston, MA: Hamilcar
  Publications, 2025.
Identifiers: ISBN: 978-1-949590-77-7 | 978-1-949590-78-4
Subjects: LCSH Boxing—Safety regulations—United States. | Boxing—
  Safety regulations. | BISAC SPORTS / Boxing
Classification: LCC KF3989 .S55 2025 | DDC 344.73/099—dc23

Paperback ISBN: 978-1949590-78-4

Hardcover ISBN: 978-1949590-77-7

hamilcarpubs.com

Aut viam inveniam aut faciam

*For my boxing mentors: Willie Grunes, Bill Goodman,
Mike Capriano Jr., and Tony Arnold. Over many years I was the
beneficiary of their deep knowledge and understanding of
a complex and often misunderstood sport.*

Contents

*The price one pays for pursuing any profession, or calling,
is an intimate knowledge of its ugly side.*
—James Baldwin

About the Cover Photo

I n May 1961 I was a sixteen-year-old boxing fanatic and an aspiring
amateur boxer, attending a fight card at the legendary St. Nicholas Arena
on West 66th Street in Manhattan. I had just purchased a new camera
and was eager to take photos of the action. The ten-round main event
featured Philadelphia's Sid "Sweet Pea" Adams versus Cuban expatriate Jose
Stable. In the sixth round Adams got knocked down. A few moments later,
with Adams trapped in a corner, the referee stopped the fight to save him
from further punishment. At the exact moment of the stoppage I happened
to snap the photo featured on the cover of this book. The story doesn't
end there, however—sadly, a featherweight boxer named Jose Rigores was
fatally injured on that same card in a six-round preliminary match. Watching
the bout from ringside, I recall that it didn't look as if Rigores was in trouble
at any time, until one punch from his opponent dropped Rigores for the full
count in round six. He then walked from the ring to his dressing room, where
he collapsed. He underwent emergency brain surgery and died a few days
later.

Call it fate, luck, or whatever, but sixty-two years later that photo I took
turned out to be the perfect cover image for this book. I hope that what I
propose here helps more boxers suffer fewer debilitating brain injuries and
avoid the fate of Jose Rigores.

**Left to Right: Jose Stable, referee Harry Ebbets, Sid "Sweet Pea" Adams,
May 29, 1961, St. Nicholas Arena, New York City.**

Introduction

I have always felt that prize fighting was a rather good sport, but I think the rules should be revised and the referees chosen with greater care. I myself have little real knowledge of the sport, but many people who I respect believe there is value in continuing the sport with proper regulation.
—Eleanor Roosevelt, 1962

In 1980 the New York State Athletic Commission mandated that an ambulance be present at every professional boxing show in the state. This mandate addressed the potential need for a fighter to be quickly transported to a hospital, especially if emergency brain surgery was necessary. It's just as important, however and of course, to do everything possible *before* and *during* the actual contest to reduce the chance that the fighter will need that ambulance.

Is enough being done to make professional boxing less dangerous? If I thought the answer to that question was "yes," this book wouldn't be necessary.

• • •

Modern boxing began in the early 1890s, with the introduction of the Marquess of Queensberry rules, which required padded leather gloves, three-minute rounds, and a minute's rest between rounds. Over the next hundred years, approximately 1,700 fighters—professional and amateur—died from injuries sustained in a boxing match.[1] From 1980 to 2023, 170 professional fighters were fatally injured.[2]

Almost all of those deaths were caused by subdural hematoma, or bleeding within the brain. The fatality count averages four professional boxers per year. You could argue that four deaths a year in a violent contact sport—in which thousands of athletes compete annually—isn't a large number. But it would be a mistake to focus solely on the number of deaths and not consider the thousands of fighters who survive their careers but suffer permanent and progressive brain damage.

Neurologic exams such as CT scans and MRIs, as well as cognitive testing both before and after fights, are useful and necessary. But no matter how thorough or sophisticated these tests are, if what happens inside the ring—during the actual fight—isn't handled properly, brain damage becomes inevitable.

Boxing can, of course, never be made completely safe. Even under the best circumstances, brain injury and death are always a possibility. That said, this book addresses circumstances that amplify the danger to fighters *unnecessarily* through a combination of abuse, negligence, and incompetence.

The book also suggests new rules and protocols that aim to reduce danger and decrease damage without detracting from boxing's inherent drama and excitement.

Chronic Traumatic Encephalopathy (CTE) is a medical term for brain damage caused by repetitive concussive and subconcussive blows to the head. What used to be known in boxing as "punch-drunk syndrome" and later "dementia pugilistica" has been relabeled CTE. Although onset and severity of symptoms vary, CTE inexorably worsens with the passage of time.

In doing research for this book, I've watched dozens of televised bouts that screamed out for intervention by the referee or ringside physician to stop the fight, yet both failed to act in time, if at all. That failure caused unnecessary brain trauma, and sometimes death.[3]

In ancient Rome, boxers who competed in the Coliseum wore gloves embedded with metal plates—each called a cestus—to make the contest more violent and deadly. Today's boxers wear padded leather gloves (usually weighing eight or ten ounces), and the contestants must follow specific rules and regulations. Yet too many contemporary professional boxing contests resemble a human demolition derby. Power and aggression are emphasized above all, and minimal attention is paid to strategy or defense. Boxing used to be called the art of self-defense, but it has become, instead, a sport of artless offense, especially since the 1990s.

I've always believed that professional boxing reflects the culture that surrounds it. In recent years many aspects of our culture have been dumbed down. Boxing is no exception. The finer points of boxing technique have been declining steadily over the past three decades. Especially troubling is the disappearance of defensive skills such as strategic use of the jab, mobile footwork, and ducking, slipping, and parrying punches aimed at the head.

The lack of quality trainers has contributed to these problems. No certification or testing program is required to become a boxing trainer, and anyone, regardless of background, can call himself a trainer. Just throw a towel over your shoulder, grab a pair of punch pads, and—poof!—you're a trainer, even though you may know less than the beginner you're instructing.

The prevalence of deficient trainers becomes clear during televised fights, when the microphone installed in a fighter's corner allows the TV audience to hear the trainer's instructions to fighters between rounds. The advice usually consists of an expletive-laced exhortation to "throw more punches . . . what are you waiting for!" Some trainers might know enough to implore the fighter to use the jab, but they can't tell him how to use it. A competent trainer can spot openings and relay that information to the fighter, but you rarely hear anything like that in the corners. It would be far more helpful if the clueless trainer simply told his boxer to "keep your hands up and chin down." (See chapter eight.)

Among the last of the old-school legendary trainers still active in the 1980s were Ray Arcel, Freddie Brown, Eddie Futch, and Cus D'Amato. Arcel and Brown, who began training boxers in the 1920s, were instrumental in refining the skills of the great lightweight champion Roberto Duran in the 1970s. Futch and D'Amato began their careers in the 1930s. In recent years two of the best trainers in the sport have been Freddie Roach and Teddy Atlas. Their teaching skills were immeasurably enhanced by having the good fortune to be mentored by, respectively, Eddie Futch and Cus D'Amato.

A NEW REALITY

We can't go back in time and expect today's champions and contenders to suddenly become clever and experienced ring technicians. In an age when boxers are winning multiple title belts with barely a dozen pro fights on their résumés—usually by defeating a similarly inexperienced opponent—any rules intended to improve boxing safety must take this new reality into account.

Unlike other professional sports, boxing has never had a national commissioner with power to limit abuses and set uniform standards. Nevertheless, there are several safety nets in place that are intended to protect the boxers' health or at least minimize the damage they suffer. But how effective are they?

It would be naïve to think that the quasi-official "sanctioning organizations" provide any kind of effective safety net.[4] The WBC, WBA, IBF, and WBO (referred to in the industry as the "Alphabet Organizations") operate independently of each other. Each recognizes its own set of champions and title contenders for boxing's seventeen weight divisions. The primary function of the Alphabets is to collect hefty sanctioning fees from every fighter who competes for one of their title belts. The Alphabets have been known to manipulate their ratings for powerful promoters, a practice that often leads to dangerous mismatches (see chapter sixteen).

Unfortunately, it's unlikely that boxing's current infrastructure will change. The present system is too entrenched, and no one has the will or motivation to correct it. Simply put, the sport's handful of dominant promoters and the four major sanctioning organizations oppose any change to boxing governance that would threaten their control over the sport.

My sole concern, as you'd expect, is for the safety of the athletes, who risk their health every time they step into a ring. If progress is to be made, the safety nets intended to protect the boxer must be fixed.

SAFETY NETS

The first safety net comprises the trainer and the manager in whose trust the boxer places his career. The second is the state or country's boxing commission. In the United States, state boxing commissions are taxpayer-funded bureaucracies headed by political appointees who collect tax revenues from fight promotions, require medical exams for boxers (although the number and type of tests varies from state to state), grant licenses and permits, approve matches, and issue suspensions for infractions.

The boxing commissions serve an essential role, but their effectiveness is often compromised by bureaucratic inefficiency and incompetence. State boxing commissioners are frequently appointed not for their expertise in boxing but rather because of political patronage, as governors often use these positions to repay political favors. This often results in poor governance and oversight of the sport.

The final safety net—the one of last resort—includes the referee and the ringside physician. (See chapters four, five, seven, and nine.)

Now, I'm not implying that professional boxers need to be treated like fragile vessels, but even the hardest steel, if overstressed, can break. A properly trained professional boxer is a superbly conditioned athlete. Years of intense training and competition harden their bodies to the point where they can absorb punches that would kill the average person. Professional boxers are a tough breed; otherwise, they wouldn't be competing in the toughest of all sports. If they've made it through several years of amateur competition, and then move up to the pros for another two or three years, that added experience should protect them from being severely injured or killed—provided they are not too abused by the incompetence and corruption that surrounds them.

Under normal circumstances it isn't easy to kill a professional boxer in the ring, but most of them will endure brain damage. The Association of Neurological Surgeons estimates that 90 percent of professional boxers suffer a brain injury during their career. The surgeons also estimate that up to 40 percent will develop symptoms of CTE after retirement, which is likely a gross underestimate.[5]

• • •

The new rules proposed in this book aim to lessen the damage and prevent life-threatening injury to boxers by patching up the holes in the safety nets.

So where do we begin? With the most urgent measure: the education and performance of referees and ringside physicians, who hold the boxer's life in their hands once the bell rings.

Other changes can and should be instituted immediately. The first is to reduce the scheduled number of rounds in a fight to make up for the inexperience and poor defensive skills shown by most contemporary boxers. With almost two hundred titles up for grabs, there are simply too many twelve-round "championship" contests involving neophyte professionals who have fought less than twenty times. Fifty or more years ago novice professional boxers would gain experience gradually in four- and six-round preliminary bouts. Abolishing twelve-round bouts would be a good start, but reducing the number of rounds even more would be a major step toward making the sport safer.

Fewer scheduled rounds may be hard for dedicated fight fans to accept, but shortening bouts has a strong historical precedent, and it didn't harm the sport. Some may dismiss the idea of shorter bouts, but I urge fans and boxing officials to consider the facts presented in chapters two and three.

Another measure that should be adopted by every boxing commission is the "standing eight count." A standing eight count occurs when the referee, at his discretion, halts action for eight seconds to assess if a boxer hit with a damaging punch—or punches—is fit to continue. I discuss the pros and cons of this rule in chapter six.

Chapter eleven explains professional boxing's current scoring system and recommends that it be modified to reward *clever* boxing while discouraging robotic and damaging slugfests.

The question of whether head guards should be mandatory is addressed in chapter twelve, and the boxing glove is scrutinized in chapter fifteen to determine if its contents, size, and weight should be changed. These topics, plus all of the new rules and protocols, are summarized in chapter nineteen.

● ● ●

I recently watched an episode of *The Twilight Zone*. The episode, titled "Steel" and starring Lee Marvin, was first broadcast in 1963. As introduced by *The Twilight Zone*'s creator Rod Serling, the fictional story takes place in 1974, "six years after professional boxing was legally abolished." Only life-size robot boxers resembling human beings were permitted to fight in the ring.

One year before the original date of that *Twilight Zone* episode, Benny "Kid" Paret and Davey Moore suffered fatal brain injuries while defending their titles. Never before had a champion been killed defending his title, let alone two champions in one year. (One of the bouts—Emile Giffith vs. Benny "Kid" Paret—was aired live on network TV.) After the two deaths, there was strong public sentiment to ban the sport, and *The Twilight Zone* script surely was influenced by these unprecedented real events.

Interestingly, Serling himself had boxed, in the army, and his first major success as a screenwriter was *Requiem for a Heavyweight*, an award-winning teleplay (1956) later made into a movie (1962). *Requiem* is a scathing portrayal of an aging and washed-up brain-damaged former heavyweight contender, Louis "Mountain" Rivera, played in the movie by Anthony Quinn and by former pro boxer Jack Palance in the television version. Some critics thought the script hackneyed and the characters one-dimensional. Serling's response was direct and to the point:

> Too much of it walked past me in the lobby of Madison Square Garden— shuffling, battered faces of "also-rans" who had left too much of themselves inside too many rings for too many years in front of too many screaming people. . . . If some of the characters who people it seem like clichés— predictable and familiar to the sport—it is because in real life they are an integral part of the habitation. There are crooks, leeches, pimps in sweatshirts, and filth in pinstriped suits; flesh peddlers and garbage collectors who trade on the Mountain Riveras, and who leave a stench more persistent than any human sweat or liniment. . . .If they seem predictable and one-dimensional, it is because there is no subtlety to a fix, a deliberate mismatch, or a selling-out of a human being for cash money.[6]

It's not clear whether Serling, despite his accurate portrayal of professional boxing, favored its abolishment, although it would appear so from his writing. But sixty years after that *Twilight Zone* episode first aired, boxing is still very much with us. Real people, not robots, are taking the punches. Huge amounts of money are generated by fans willing to pay to watch two human beings fight each other.

Calls for boxing's abolition are no longer as strong as they were sixty or more years ago, when the sport was still an important part of American popular culture. As a young fan and for many years after, although aware of the danger boxers face, I vehemently opposed any law that would have abolished the sport. Boxing has been a huge part of my life, but my enjoyment of it has waned. And it is not just the lack of nuance and skill, or the confusion of having so many bogus titles generated by a gaggle of ridiculous sanctioning organizations that has lessened my enthusiasm. More importantly, I can no longer ignore or abide the terrible damage inflicted upon the brains of these modern-day gladiators.

The Twilight Zone notwithstanding, professional boxing won't be abolished. The new rules proposed in this book, if adopted, will benefit current and future generations of boxers by keeping them safer and healthier. It's now up to those who control the professional boxing industry to decide whether to keep the status quo or do the right thing and make the changes that this ancient sport desperately needs.

CHAPTER 1

A Brief History

As much as I love boxing, I hate it, and as much as I hate it,
I love it. Every sensitive aficionado of the sport must bring to it this
ambivalence. For make no mistake about it, at its worst, professional
boxing is a cruel sport, just as, at its best, it is exhilarating, artistic
and, yes, ennobling. A natural rivalry between two gifted professionals,
tuned to perfection, is, in this opinion, a sporting event surpassing
all others, from Super Bowls to Kentucky Derbies.
—Budd Schulberg

Boxing is an ancient sport steeped in tradition. History has shown that change in it does not come easily—especially when it comes to safety measures. Indeed, as this chapter will reveal, rules generally remain unchanged for decades.

Modern boxing's progenitor began in England in the late 17th century, with the appearance of bare-knuckle prizefights. It wasn't until 1743 that England's Jack Broughton, the most celebrated pugilist of his age, became the first person to codify a set of rules.

Broughton's rules were intended primarily to introduce some order for gambling purposes. In addition to allowing punches, the rules allowed contestants to use wrestling maneuvers to throw an opponent to the ground, provided the opponent was grabbed above the waist.

A round ended when one of the contestants was thrown or punched to the ground. The downed fighter was to be assisted or carried back to his corner

A two-thousand-year-old bronze statue of a boxer discovered in 1885 during an excavation for an apartment building in Rome, Italy. *Photograph by Sol Kirby*

by his seconds and given thirty seconds to recover before he returned to his side of the "scratch mark"—a yard square marked out in the middle of the ring—to begin another round. If the fighter could not "come up to scratch" or "toe the mark," he was considered "knocked out of time" (in modern parlance, simply "knocked out") and declared the loser.

Perhaps Broughton's greatest contribution to the sport, however, was his invention of modern boxing gloves, which he called "mufflers." Boxing historians believe the mufflers were stuffed with either horsehair or lamb's wool. They were used for training, instruction, and sparring exhibitions. The fights themselves continued to be fought with bare knuckles. Mufflers were provided to Broughton's students, many of whom came from the upper classes and aristocracy, with the assurance they would provide protection "from the Inconveniency of black Eyes, broken Jaws, and bloody Noses [sic]."[7]

All bare-knuckle contests were "finish fights," which had no time limit and could only end when a boxer quit, was knocked out of time, or was disqualified for fouling. Bare-knuckle fights ran the gamut from the insufferably boring—involving much wrestling and stalling—to the extremely savage, bloody, and sometimes fatal. Because fights had no time limit, they could end in minutes or last several hours. (The longest bare-knuckle fight on record is said to have lasted six hours and fifteen minutes.) Strength, endurance, aggressive rushing, and brute force predominated, especially in the early days of bare-knuckle fighting. Significant weight differences between combatants were not unusual, particularly because the weight classes were few and ill defined.

Broughton's rules remained virtually unaltered for nearly a hundred years, until they were superseded by the "New Rules" of 1838, which followed the death of William Phelps after his contest with Owen Swift. (Swift was the only bare-knuckle champion to have killed two opponents.) To bring greater safety and order to the sport, one new rule stipulated that a downed fighter be given eight additional seconds—after the initial thirty-second respite—to reach, *unaided*, a mark in the center of the ring. If he could not reach the mark, he was considered beaten. This rule prevented seconds from carrying an exhausted or semiconscious fighter to the scratch—an innovation that was thought to save lives. Specified fouls in the New Rules included head-butting, hitting below the belt, gouging, biting, scratching, and striking a downed opponent (this last one existed in Broughton's rules).[8]

Bare-knuckle fights were often bloody and brutal. Tom Sayers (right) knocked out Tom Paddock for the championship of England in 1858. *Author's collection*

In the decades after the peak years—1785-1825—of bare-knuckle prize-fighting in England, betting scandals, fixed fights, and widely reported ring fatalities fueled a growing movement to abolish the sport. In addition to these problems, crowd control was generally poor at prizefights, allowing pickpockets and ruffians to roam freely among the spectators. Disgruntled gamblers and spectators would sometimes rush the ring to force an end to the contest if their man appeared on the verge of losing. As a result, wealthy patrons, including the aristocracy, became disillusioned and withdrew their support. It had become obvious that if pugilism were to survive as a popular spectator sport, it needed to reinvent itself.

The solution came with the adoption of the Marquess of Queensberry rules. They are believed to have been created for amateur boxing in 1867, although the actual date when they were framed hasn't been established conclusively. The Queensberry rules were written by the Welsh sportsman John Graham Chambers and endorsed publicly by the eighth (now considered ninth) Marquess of Queensberry, John Sholto Douglas. Whether the Marquess himself contributed anything to the rules, however, is a matter of debate. The gradual adoption of the rules for professional boxing followed in due course; and with minor adjustments, these same rules govern boxing today.

Notably, the Queensberry rules limited rounds to three minutes each, followed by one minute of rest. Throwing or wrestling an opponent to the ground was outlawed, and the rules stated that a boxer who was knocked down by a punch had ten seconds to get up or be counted out and lose the match.

While the new rules also required gloves, it took more than two decades after their framing for gloved bouts to be fully accepted by fighters, fans, and sportswriters (and even then, the occasional traditionalist remained unconvinced). The preeminent bare-knuckle boxing historian Tony Gee explains:

> [Bare-knuckle boxing] certainly did not disappear overnight. Whilst some were apparently ready to embrace the gloved approach, others appeared to agree with *Tinsley's Magazine* that there "is a certain make-believe in the glove-business which quite unfits it for comparison with the real thing."

Gee notes that some contemporary sporting publications considered all but bare-knuckle fights "mere travesties of the original." In 1887, so he writes, "*The Sporting Life* [newspaper] was still seeing gloved bouts as a mere learning experience for bare-knuckle combat, declaring that anybody 'standing on the very lowest rung of the ladder of common sense should be aware that boxing with the mittens is intended as a preliminary to using the raw material.'"[9]

The required use of padded leather gloves—usually weighing between two to five ounces—was the most revolutionary of the Queensberry rules. Padded gloves served two purposes: While they gave some protection to fighters' hands, they also added the illusion of safety, giving the impression that boxing was now less dangerous than the bare-knuckle version. Ironically, by reducing the impact of a punch on a boxer's hands and knuckles, the wearing of gloves actually created greater potential for serious injury. As author and sports historian Elliott J. Gorn notes:

> Gloves protected fighters' hands more than their heads, added weight to each punch, and allowed men to throw innumerable blows to such hard-but-vulnerable spots as the temples and jaw. . . . In addition, the new ten-second knockout rule further encouraged clubbing blows, because it

was much easier to punch a man into ten seconds than into thirty seconds of unconsciousness. . . . Above all the Queensberry rules emphasized quick, dramatic blows. In important respects, boxing became simpler and faster-paced, essential qualities if it was to appeal to a wide if not particularly knowledgeable audience.[10]

As Gorn implies, the transition from bare-knuckle to Queensberry rules required adjustments in style and strategy. The elimination of wrestling served to focus attention on boxing technique. Most bare-knuckle fights had been contested on turf that required shoes with spikes. A canvas-covered wooden platform required leather-soled athletic footwear, which increased the speed and mobility of footwork. Another major change was the addition of new weight classifications. By the early 1900s, there were eight internationally recognized weight divisions, which ranged from flyweight (limit 112 pounds) to heavyweight (over 175 pounds).

The last bare-knuckle heavyweight championship took place on July 8, 1889, at Richburg, Mississippi. The legendary "Boston Strong Boy," John L. Sullivan, defended his widely recognized title against Jake Kilrain, who held the *Police Gazette* belt. Sullivan retained his title when Kilrain's cornerman, fearing for his fighter's life, threw in the sponge before the seventy-sixth round. The fight had lasted more than two hours under a broiling southern sun.

The old bare-knuckle era essentially ended in New Orleans on September 7, 1892. On that date, in a contest fought under Marquess of Queensberry rules, James J. Corbett ("Gentleman Jim") upset the odds, knocking Sullivan out in the twenty-first round of a fight to the finish. Corbett was seven years younger than the thirty-three-year-old Sullivan, whose best days were behind him. Significantly, the new champion, wearing five-ounce leather gloves, hit his opponent countless times without severely damaging his hands.

Corbett, a former San Francisco bank clerk, had never engaged in a bare-knuckle bout. All his previous contests were conducted under the Queensberry rules. At the time his evasive and mobile style was a novelty for a heavyweight boxer. It emphasized speed, footwork, ducking, feinting, counterpunching, and strategic use of the left jab. Corbett's historic victory over Sullivan was a triumph of brains over brawn, and it set a template for all boxers who followed. Corbett's style allowed for aggression, but

July 8, 1889, Richburg, Mississippi. "The Boston Strong Boy," John L. Sullivan (left), defeated Jake Kilrain in the last bare-knuckle heavyweight championship. *Library of Congress*

not at the expense of one's defense. The conqueror of "The Great John L." influenced many other fighters to adopt a more "cerebral" approach to the game.

For a time "fights to the finish," even under Queensberry rules, were still in vogue. The most famous was Corbett's epic battle with the great Australian champion Peter Jackson, the first notable Black heavyweight of the gloved era. On May 21, 1891, in San Francisco, they fought an incredible sixty-one three-minute rounds, more than three hours of fighting. The first thirty rounds featured lively exchanges, but after that, with both men fatigued, the pace slowed considerably. At the end of round sixty-one, with the exhausted boxers barely moving, the referee stopped the fight and declared it a "no contest," which canceled all bets.

The Corbett–Jackson sixty-one-round marathon paled in comparison to the 1893 fight between lightweights Andy Bowen and Jack Burke in New Orleans. They fought the longest fight ever, at seven hours and twenty minutes (110 three-minute rounds). It was reported that the fight went on so long that most spectators who stayed to the end had long since fallen asleep in their seats. From round 105 on, the exhausted fighters just circled each other without throwing punches. With both men too dazed and damaged to come out of their corners for the 111th round, the referee declared a "no contest" that later was changed to a "draw."[11] Less than two years later, Bowen was fatally injured in a bout against Kid Lavigne.

During this time, the sport was adjusting and evolving, finding its way from bare-knuckle fights to Queensberry rules. Finish fights were eventually phased out, replaced for a time by contests scheduled for twenty-five or forty-five rounds. But these time-limited marathon fights were the exception, not the rule.

It could take months for a fighter to recuperate from a particularly grueling marathon bout. Most fighters preferred to go six, eight, or ten rounds. Shorter contests allowed for a more active fight schedule, and that meant less time between paydays. By the 1910s, though twenty-round bouts were not uncommon, most professional bouts were limited to ten rounds or fewer. Some locales restricted bouts to four or six rounds, as was the case in California (four-round limit from 1914 to 1925) and Philadelphia (six-round limit from 1900 to 1920). Interestingly, boxing remained popular in both places despite the shorter bouts. (See chapter three.)

The marathon mentality eventually disappeared, and the tempo of fights accelerated. Fighters no longer needed to "coast" for several rounds to conserve energy, as was often the case in bouts that exceeded twenty rounds. The typical bare-knuckle style of boxing—primarily moving toward your opponent in a straight line and throwing mostly single punches—didn't work for shorter fights. The early Queensberry fighters, most notably those in lighter weight divisions, realized that constant movement gave them more chances to set up a variety of combinations.

At the same time that the modern style of boxing was emerging, the sport was gaining greater public acceptance in the United States. During World War I, boxing was used to entertain and to condition recruits preparing to go overseas. Boxing abolitionists and allied politicians found it increasingly difficult to mount an effective attack.

Beginning in the 1880s and continuing into the next century, the American boxing scene was in ascendance, fueled by the influx of millions of poor immigrants from southern and eastern Europe into rapidly industrializing cities.

By the first decade of the 20th century, the United States had become the center of the sport and home to most of its champions. Boxing had successfully metamorphosed into a huge and successful part of the entertainment industry and was about to realize its full potential as a mainstream spectator sport.

In 1921, boxing became the first sport to draw over a million dollars for a single event, when Jack Dempsey successfully defended his heavyweight championship against France's Georges Carpentier. The new medium of radio and movie newsreels of the era's greatest fights increased the sport's popularity. Boxing became even more popular when television became available to the general public in the late 1940s, making it possible for millions of new fans to watch "the fights" nearly every night of the week. In the 1950s, boxing reportedly sold as many television sets as the popular television comic Milton Berle, and rivaled the hit show *I Love Lucy* in the ratings.[12]

But the specter of tragedy in the ring hovered over the sport. In the early 1950s, after two boxers were fatally injured in televised fights emanating from New York City, several new safety measures were added to the New

1923. Yankee Stadium. Luis Angel Firpo and Jack McAuliffe swap punches in front of 87,000 fans. During the Roaring Twenties boxing rivaled baseball in popularity. *Author's collection*

York State Athletic Commission's rule book. First, if a fighter suffered a loss by knockout, he wasn't allowed to fight again for thirty days. Second, three knockdowns in any one round would automatically end the fight (a rule since rescinded in New York and other states). And third, a new rule—adopted universally—stated that a knocked down boxer could no longer be saved by the bell in any round. In other words, if the boxer is still down when the bell rings to end the round, the count will continue until the boxer either rises or is counted out. No doubt these rules saved lives, but, as we shall see, there was still much room for improvement.

In 1976 television viewers saw five American boxers win gold medals at the Montreal Olympics. That same year the blockbuster movie *Rocky* generated renewed interest in the sport. Before the decade ended, boxing was back on network television on a regular basis after a twelve-year hiatus. Notable during the 1980s was the great rivalry between boxing's "Four Kings"—Sugar Ray Leonard, Tommy Hearns, Marvin Hagler, and Roberto Duran.

THE NEW MILLENNIUM: A TRANSFORMATIVE TIME FOR BOXING

A decade later, cable television and pay-per-view became the predominant outlets for boxing. In the coming years, these media would be joined by on-demand internet streaming services—DAZN, ESPN+, and Sky TV, among others. Nevertheless, by the second decade of the 21st century boxing had become a fringe sport compared to professional baseball, football, and basketball. And there was competition from the new sport of Mixed Martial Arts (MMA) as well. The rare superfight, however, could still generate huge interest. In 2015, ninety-four years after the Dempsey–Carpentier fight, a pay-per-view audience of 4.4 million paid more than $400 million to watch Floyd Mayweather Jr. outpoint Manny Pacquiao for the welterweight championship. Mayweather earned over $200 million and Pacquiao approximately $120 million. Boxing has not seen an event that drew more global attention or generated more money since that fight, which also remains significant for matching the two best fighters of a generation, even though the match occurred when both were slightly past their primes.[13]

Meanwhile, the rise of social media has had a profound impact on boxing, as evidenced by the success of Jake Paul, an American social-media influencer and actor turned professional boxer. Before he became a boxer, Paul had more than twenty million followers on his YouTube channel and nearly seventeen million on Instagram. Over the past four and a half years, he's compiled a 10-1 record but hasn't yet beaten a real professional boxer. On August 5, 2023, Paul won an eight-round decision over veteran MMA fighter Nate Diaz, who was making his boxing debut. The match reportedly drew 500,000 pay-per-view buyers in the United States at $60 a pop, which added up to $30 million.[14]

On November 15, 2024, at the AT&T Stadium, in Arlington, Texas, Paul, twenty-seven, fought the fifty-eight-year-old former heavyweight champion Mike Tyson. Broadcast on Netflix, the fight, Tyson's first in nineteen years, aroused interest across the world. Paul made an estimated $40 million for the fight, double Tyson's $20 million. After eight tame two-minute rounds, Jake Paul was awarded a unanimous decision.

Obviously, the sport is evolving—some would say devolving—because of the power of social media.

Jake Paul's entry into professional boxing is a sideshow—albeit a lucrative one—but it may be a sign of things to come. Exactly how boxing will change and adjust over the next ten years is anyone's guess (see chapter eighteen), but what will never change is the brutal and bloody confrontational nature of the sport, and what happens when a gloved fist collides with the human skull.

CHAPTER 2

The Case for Shorter Fights—Part I: What the Statistics Reveal

It is quality rather than quantity that matters.
—Seneca

T he year 2019 wasn't a good one for pro boxing. On October 12, at Chicago's Wintrust Arena, a promising twenty-seven-year-old boxer named Patrick Day suffered a fatal brain injury while fighting his twenty-second bout. Day was the fourth professional boxer in four months to die from punishment taken in the ring. On top of that in the same year five other boxers were rushed to hospitals and had to undergo emergency brain surgery to remove blood clots in their brain.[15]

• • •

Patrick Day turned professional in 2013, compiling a 12-2-1 record (including six wins by knockout) in his first four years. Up to then Day had never gone beyond eight rounds. In his sixteenth pro bout, he fought his first ten rounder, winning a unanimous decision. In his next bout—also ten rounds—he won the World Boxing Council (WBC) Continental Americas Super Welterweight Championship. Winning this minor title ensured that all his future fights would be scheduled for ten or twelve rounds. After defeating two of his next three opponents on points, Day fought Charles Conwell, a boxer with eleven wins, including eight by knockout, and no losses. Conwell also held a championship of sorts: the International Boxing Federation (IBF) USBA Super Welterweight title.

Day was knocked down in the fourth round of the Conwell fight and again in the eighth by right-hand punches to his head. He was behind in the scoring, having won only two of the previous seven rounds. After the bell rang to end the eighth round before action could resume following the knockdown, the TV commentator noted that, "Day wobbled back to his corner."

I don't know if any of the four ringside physicians assigned by the Illinois State Boxing Commission entered the ring to examine Day during the one-minute rest period between the eighth and ninth rounds. Either way, it's questionable whether Day was fit to answer the bell for round nine. Because the YouTube video of the fight only includes selected highlights, the ninth round is missing, so we do not know how much punishment Day took during its three minutes.

The video resumes at the beginning of the tenth round. Eighty seconds into it, Day was hit with another right that staggered him. Retreating on unsteady legs, he was hit by two quick follow-up punches that knocked him backward and down. The back of Day's head slammed hard against the ring floor. Day underwent emergency brain surgery for a subdural hematoma. He never regained consciousness and died four days later.[16]

• • •

The fatal brain bleed could have begun in the eighth or ninth round, or with the punches that staggered and dropped him in the tenth, or when his head violently hit the ring floor. We just don't know. What we do know is that if Patrick Day were fighting fifty or more years ago, his apprenticeship in the professional ranks would have put him on a different trajectory. He would not have been fighting ten-round main events with barely a dozen pro fights under his belt. His fight with Conwell would have been scheduled for six or eight rounds. There is no guarantee, of course, that a six or eight-round fight would have made a difference to the outcome. What *is* certain is that Patrick Day would have been spared the punishment he absorbed in rounds nine and ten, and that likely would have made the difference between life and death.

Three months earlier, on July 19, in a fight at the MGM National Harbor Hotel & Casino in Oxon Hill, Maryland, twenty-eight-year-old Maxim Dadashev fought Subriel Matias in a twelve-round IBF light-welterweight title elimination bout. Going into the bout, Dadashev was undefeated in thirteen pro fights, winning eleven by knockout. Matias was also undefeated in thirteen fights, with all of his wins coming by knockout.

Up to the seventh round the Dadashev–Matias fight was even, but after that Dadashev began to wilt under Matias' incessant pressure. The punishment increased in succeeding rounds, with Matias easily winning rounds eight through eleven, as he consistently landed hard punches on the exhausted Russian boxer's head and body. By this time, the fight was no longer competitive.

Between the eleventh and twelfth rounds, Buddy McGirt, a former world champion and Dadashev's trainer, asked the referee to stop the uneven contest. McGirt later said that he had considered stopping the bout two rounds earlier because he felt his fighter was fading and taking too many punches.[17]

Dadashev collapsed after exiting the ring. He died four days later, after being hospitalized in critical condition and undergoing emergency brain surgery for a subdural hematoma.

● ● ●

Neither Patrick Day nor Maxim Dadashev should have been fighting in a bout of more than eight rounds. In fact, a six-round bout would have been more appropriate, given their skill levels and experience. In decades past, they would not have been rated among their division's top ten contenders, let alone been fighting for a title.

Dadashev, with thirteen professional bouts, and Day, with twenty-one, weren't ready for a punishing ten-round or twelve-round bout at this early stage of their professional boxing careers. In both fights, the most severe punishment was meted out after the seventh round, as the inexperienced fighters became increasingly fatigued. Knowing how to properly pace yourself for a longer bout is a skill that comes with experience. Day and Dadashev's inexperience likely contributed to their deaths. Compounding the danger for both fighters was the incompetence of the referees and ringside physicians, who should have intervened and stopped the fights no later than the ninth round, and probably before it.

Do these tragedies, and similar ones documented throughout this book, justify limiting the number of scheduled rounds for all professional boxing contests? With boxers' defensive skills at an all-time low and hundreds of inexperienced boxers subjecting their brains to unnecessary trauma, limiting the number of rounds is not only justifiable, but essential. The statistics below support this premise.

A study published in the January 2022 issue of the *Journal of Combat Sports Medicine*, published by the Association of Ringside Physicians (ARP), determined that eighty-four professional boxers were fatally injured in the ring from 2000 to 2019 (Figure 1a).[18] The study was restricted to male professional boxers whose brain injuries were sustained directly from competition.

The ARP study found that fifty-eight of eighty-two fights in question (71 percent of them) ended between the sixth- and twelfth rounds.[19] (Rounds are on the horizontal line in Figure 1b.) Two of the eighty-four bouts were excluded from this statistic because their final round could not be verified through BoxRec.com (indicated by a question mark in the graph).

Not all the fights ended in a KO or TKO—twenty went to a decision, and two were draws. The twenty fighters who lasted the scheduled distance collapsed shortly after the final bell ended the match, including one fighter who was awarded the decision.

The data revealed that twenty-seven of the eighty-two fights (33 percent) ending in a KO or TKO occurred in the last scheduled round.[20] (In professional boxing bouts are scheduled for four, six, eight, ten, or twelve rounds.)

Figure 1a. Deaths per Year, 2000 to 2019

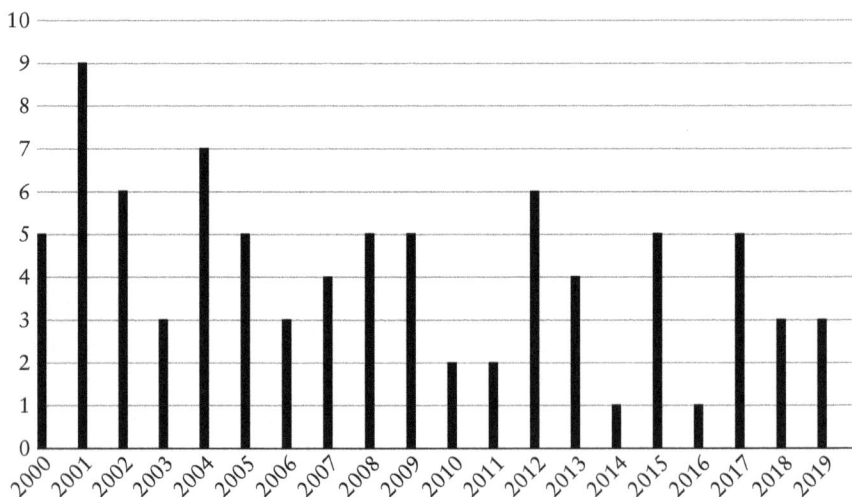

Figure 1b. Deaths by Round, 2000 to 2019

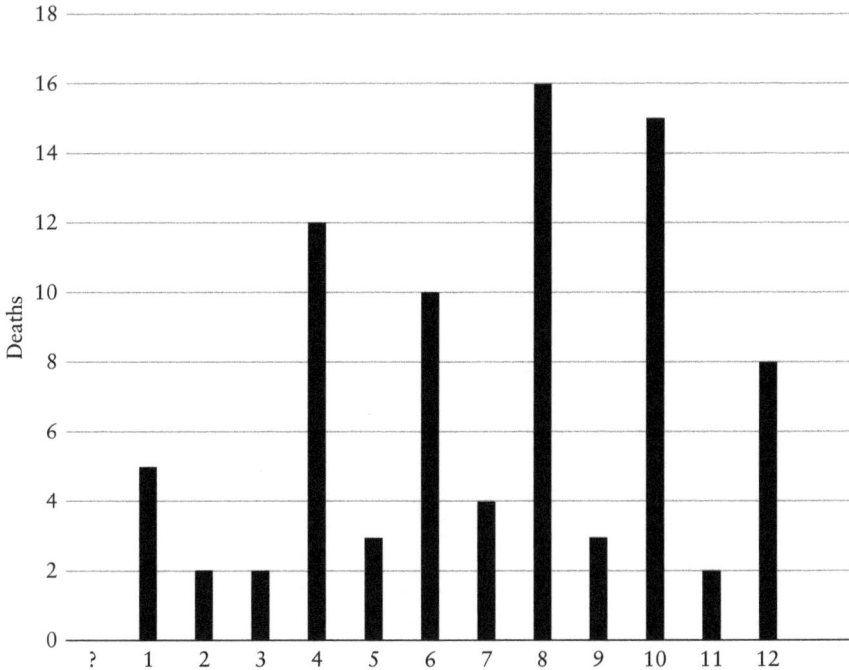

Another important finding was that sixty-two (75 percent) of eighty-three fatalities involved fighters who weighed between 108 and 135 pounds. See Table 1. (One fighter's weight was undetermined.) According to BoxRec .com, 43 percent of all known professional bouts from 2000 to 2019 involved fighters in the lightweight class (135 pounds) or lower.[21] The study offered no explanation for the disproportionally higher number of deaths in the lighter weight divisions, but it is possible that fighters weighing between 108 and 135 pounds average more punches per round than their heavier counterparts, resulting in more sustained and repetitive head punishment. The punches of lighter-weight fighters may not look as heavy or powerful as a middleweight's or heavyweight's, but they may be doing more damage because of their number.

The higher number of deaths in the lighter divisions could also be explained by the fact that most fighters weighing between 108 and 135 pounds come from countries such as the Philippines, Mexico, South Africa, and Indonesia. Of the eighty-four fatalities, 78.5 percent occurred in third world countries where safety protocols are often inadequate. Many venues in these countries

Table 1. Deaths by Weight Class

Weight Class	Limit (lbs.)	2000–2019	1980–1999
Light flyweight	108	7	4
Flyweight	112	9	10
Super flyweight	115	7	4
Bantamweight	118	5	4
Super bantamweight	122	7	7
Featherweight	126	12	10
Super featherweight	130	6	5
Lightweight	135	9	10
Super lightweight	140	7	2
Welterweight	147	4	6
Super welterweight	154	1	2
Middleweight	160	1	4
Super middleweight	168	0	4
Light heavyweight	175	4	1
Cruiserweight	200	1	0
Heavyweight	Over 200	3	0
Total		83	73

do not have an ambulance on-site, which delays getting the injured fighter to a hospital with modern diagnostic tools and qualified specialists.

If you compare the data for 2000 to 2019 to comparable data for 1980 to 1999, you see consistent trends in pro boxers' deaths caused by head injuries. From 1980 to 1999 seventy-six pro fights ended with a fatality (Figure 2a).[22] (Three fatal fights—two in Indonesia and one in Mexico— were not included in the count because fighter's weights and number of rounds could not be verified.)

Of the seventy-six remaining matches, sixty-five (86 percent) went past the fifth round (indicated by the horizontal line in Figure 2b), whereas 71 percent of fatal fights between 2000 and 2019 went past the fifth round.

Twelve of the seventy-six fatal fights between 1980 and 1999 went to a decision, including one draw. Two fighters who outpointed their opponents became unconscious before leaving the ring. Another collapsed after knocking out his opponent in the sixth round. As happens very rarely, one fighter who fatally injured his opponent himself suffered a fatal brain bleed in a subsequent match.

Fifty-four (71 percent) of the seventy-six fighters who died between 1980 and 1999 weighed 108 to 135 pounds, slightly more than ten percentage points lower than the figures for 2000 to 2019 (see Table 1). The data for both

Table 2. Deaths by Number of Career Bouts, 2000 to 2019

Career Bouts	Deaths
Pro Debut	13
1 to 5	17
6 to 10	10
11 to 15	15
16 to 20	7
21 to 25	10
26 to 30	4
31 to 35	1
36 to 40	5
40+	2
Total	84

Figure 2a. Deaths per Year, 1980 to 1999

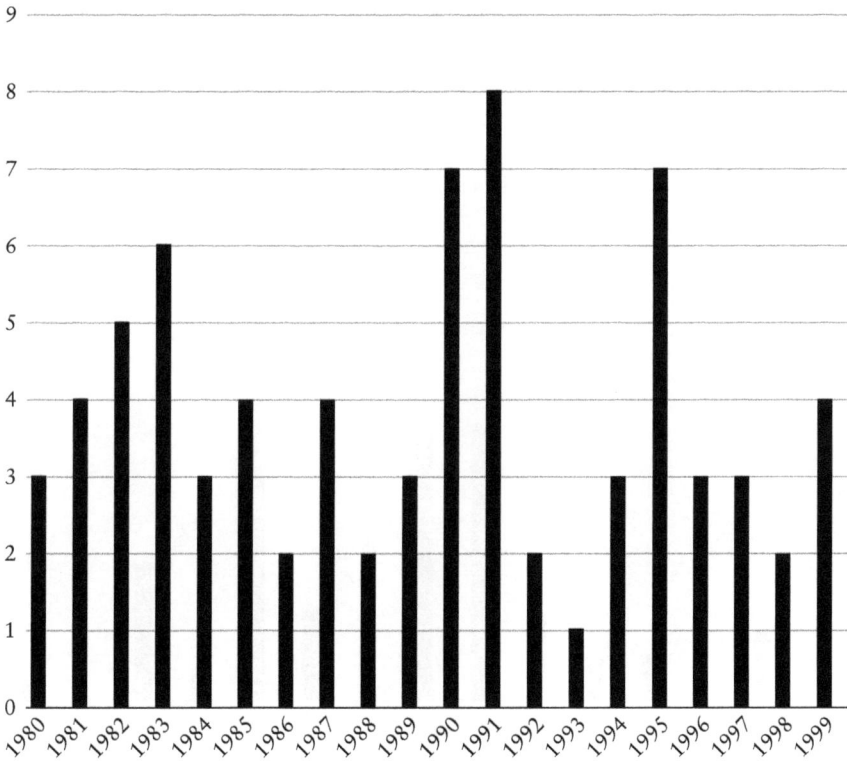

time frames (2000 to 2019 and 1980 to 1999) indicate that fighters weighing at or below 135 pounds are at greater risk. In both eras 78 percent of the fatal fights took place in less developed countries.

As noted earlier, 33 percent of the fatal bouts from 2000 to 2019 ended in a KO or TKO in the last scheduled round. Between 1980 and 1999, 32 percent ended by KO or TKO in the last scheduled round.

The statistics also reveal that inexperienced fighters are at greater risk. Sixty-six (86 percent) boxers killed in the ring during 1980–1999 had twenty-five bouts or fewer going into the fatal bout (Table 3). The figure for 2000–2019 is 73 percent (Table 2). Both percentages show that inexperienced fighters are being rushed into longer bouts too early in their careers.

Over the four years between 2020 and 2023, ten fighters were fatally injured during a pro boxing match. Seven of the ten bouts (70 percent) continued past the fifth round. Two went to a decision. One fight ended in the third round, when a thirty-eight-year-old boxer reportedly suffered a heart attack (which is extremely rare in a pro boxing match). Knockouts occurred in rounds three, four, six, seven, eight (twice), and ten. Included in the dead was eighteen-year-old Jeanette Zacarias Zapata, the second female professional boxer to be killed in the ring. Less than three months earlier, Zapata had been knocked out and was unconscious for several minutes. In her final bout, the woefully

Figure 2b. Deaths by Round, 1980 to 1999

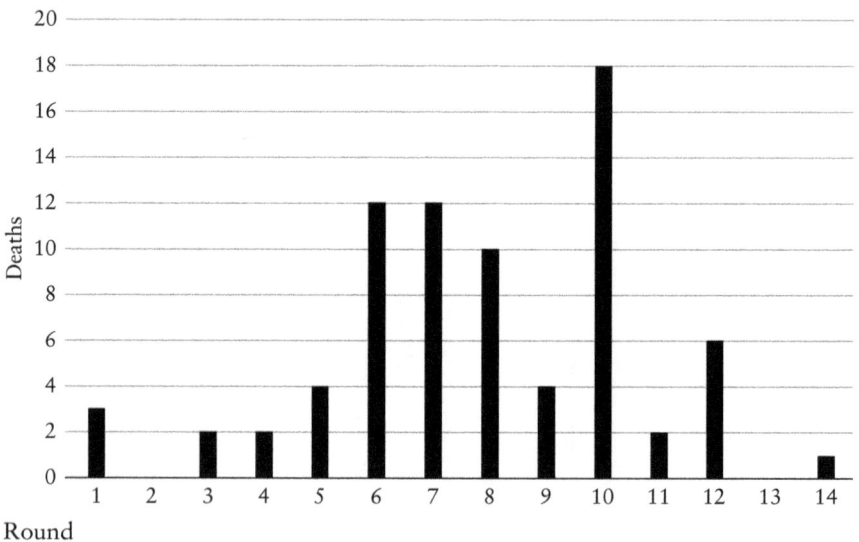

Table 3. Deaths by Number of Career Bouts, 1980 to 1999

Career Bouts	Deaths
Pro Debut	11
1 to 5	15
6 to 10	13
11 to 15	12
16 to 20	11
21 to 25	5
26 to 30	1
31 to 35	3
36 to 40	4
40+	1
Total	76

inexperienced and horribly mismanaged teenager was thrown in with an undefeated thirty-one-year-old former amateur champion.[23]

It is important to note that all these boxers were relatively inexperienced. Eight had had fewer than ten pro fights. Two had had between ten and twenty fights. One had had only four fights (for a total of thirteen rounds). Two of the boxers who made it to the eighth round had had only twenty-five fights and thirty-three rounds of previous experience. The situation cries out for a new rule that would ban bouts beyond six rounds for fighters with fewer than fifty professional rounds.

Although the data from 2020–2023 represent a small sample, the statistics are consistent with observations from the previous forty years. Both show that most fatalities occur after the fifth round, with greater danger for inexperienced boxers and those weighing between 108 and 135 pounds.

● ● ●

I realize I've given you a lot of data to take in, but the data provide important lessons. You can infer, of course, that the longer a fight continues, the more a boxer gets hit with punches to the head. Inexperience, fatigue, and the effects of dehydration all weaken defense. The fifth round appears to be an important demarcation point for boxing safety: From 1990 to 2023, more than 70 percent of 170 fights that resulted in a fatality continued past that round.

The final scheduled round of a fight appears to be particularly dangerous. The final scheduled round gives the boxer one last opportunity to impress the judges or—if he's behind on the scorecards—try for a knockout. Even in amateur fights, fatalities peak in the final round of a three-round contest.[24] Cornermen often implore their fighter to go all out in the last round. Referees, for their part, may hesitate to stop a fight in the last scheduled round, feeling pressure to give the fighters a chance to make it to the bell. This frame of mind is dangerous. Referees and ringside physicians must be taught that the last round of a bout is the most dangerous one for both fighters. As the end of the fight approaches, the referee can't have one eye on the ring clock and one eye on the fighters.

● ● ●

A fighter who hasn't fought in a year or more is also cause for concern. Extended layoffs—which are common today—affect timing and physical conditioning. A fighter coming off a long layoff is at a disadvantage when facing a more active opponent. In this scenario, limiting the number of rounds would help level the playing field and reduce the probability of injury. Those deciding on the appropriate number of rounds should consider the length of the layoff, the fighter's in-ring history, and his experience level.

An egregious example of the danger of longer fights involving recently inactive fighters occurred on October 16, 2021, in the WBC's backyard of Cancun, Mexico. Former champion Moises Fuentes (25-6-1) was launching an ill-advised comeback at age thirty-six after having retired three years earlier. Compounding these issues was the fact that before Fuentes retired he'd lost four out of five fights, the last two by knockout.

Instead of being put into an easy tune-up fight to test his reflexes and improve his timing, Fuentes was thrown into a ten-round title fight for something called the "WBC Youth Silver Flyweight Title." His opponent, nineteen-year-old David Contreras, one of the flyweight division's hottest prospects, was undefeated in nineteen fights, including seventeen that he won by knockout.

Fuentes's poor timing and rusty reflexes made him an easy target for his opponent's punches. Contreras dominated the fight, winning the first five rounds. In the sixth round a left hook to the jaw dropped Fuentes hard. The back of his head slammed against the ring floor. The unconscious boxer left the ring on a stretcher. At the hospital, he underwent brain surgery. He never regained consciousness and succumbed to his injuries a month later.

Considering his age, his two previous losses by knockout, and his three full years of inactivity, Fuentes should not even have been granted a license to fight. But Fuentes might still have survived the fight if it had been limited to five rounds.

• • •

Now for some anecdotal evidence. I have interviewed dozens of retired professional boxers, including several who fought in the 1920s and 1930s. Some were terribly damaged, while others appeared less so. The fighters whose records were made up almost entirely of six- and eight-round bouts and were considered better than average, appeared to be less damaged, even though they may have had more than fifty professional fights. The less-damaged fighters I interviewed had another thing in common: quitting at a young age—usually their mid-twenties—and while still in their prime. They may not have escaped entirely unscathed, but they didn't exhibit any outward signs of CTE, and this includes two who lived well into their eighties. I believe that the shorter length of all their fights had something to do with it.

I am not suggesting that every professional fight be limited to five rounds, even though according to the statistics that is the optimal distance for safety. Ideally, each match should be assessed responsibly on its merits before officials decide the number of rounds. There are circumstances where a six-, eight-, or ten-round bout can be considered acceptable. But the mere fact that an Alphabet belt or eliminator is on the line doesn't mean that the fighters should be automatically put into a ten- or twelve-round bout. And yet it happens repeatedly, often with disastrous results.

Shortening the scheduled distance for most professional boxing matches will not eliminate brain damage or even death, but it can reduce the incidence of both. Fewer rounds can save an inexperienced, exhausted, dehydrated, or overmatched boxer from additional damage that is often exacerbated by poor refereeing and inadequately trained or hesitant ringside physicians.

But the question remains: Can we strike a balance between safety and fan acceptance? When trial lawyers want to buttress their argument and make their case to the jury, they will often cite a "precedent" (a legal ruling in a similar case). As explained in the next chapter, there is a strong historical and legal precedent for mandating shorter fights without reducing boxing's popularity.

CHAPTER 3

The Case for Shorter Fights—Part II: Learning from the Past

The farther backward you can look, the farther forward you are likely to see.
—Winston Churchill

Controversy over the length of professional prizefights is nothing new. In the 1890s the Marquess of Queensberry rules revolutionized the sport by requiring gloves and limiting rounds to three minutes separated by one minute of rest. But no provision was made for how long a contest should last. Under the old bare-knuckle rules a fight could end only by surrender, disqualification, or knockout. Some of the earliest Queensberry fights maintained that tradition and didn't limit the number of scheduled rounds.

Over the next quarter century, professional prizefights conducted under the new Queensberry rules varied from four to twenty-five rounds, with some championship bouts scheduled for forty-five rounds. The last forty-five-round heavyweight title fight was Jack Johnson–Jess Willard, in 1915. Willard knocked out Johnson in the twenty-sixth round, in Havana, Cuba.

During the first two decades of the 20th century, many states and municipalities banned professional boxing outright, while others allowed it but with restrictions. Two major boxing venues, the state of California and the city of Philadelphia, limited fights to four or six rounds to pacify reformers and gain greater public acceptance. In the 1920s both California and Philadelphia raised the limit to ten rounds. Illinois adopted the ten-round limit a few years later. Thus, the famous Jack Dempsey–Gene Tunney heavyweight championship fights, in Philadelphia and Chicago in 1926 and 1927, were limited to ten rounds.

Other ring legends who fought in title fights limited to ten rounds included Joe Louis, Benny Leonard, Mickey Walker, Tommy Loughran, Henry Armstrong, Barney Ross, Tony Canzoneri, Jackie "Kid" Berg, and Kid Chocolate. In the 1930s, forty-nine world title fights (about 20 percent of the total number of title fights for the decade) were limited to ten rounds.[25] During the Golden Age of televised boxing, from 1950 to 1964, nearly two thousand nontitle main events broadcast locally or nationally were contested at the ten-round limit. The public never felt cheated as shown by the consistently high television ratings.

THE PHILADELPHIA SIX-ROUND RULE

In the 1890s, Philadelphia had a reputation as one of the leading fight centers of the world. But the deaths of two boxers there aroused progressive reformers and legislators, who saw an opportunity to exploit the controversy and call for the sport to be abolished in the city. In 1900, in response to the pressure, the city's public safety director limited all professional contests in Philadelphia to four rounds. A few years later, the limit was raised to six rounds. (Other Pennsylvania cities made up their own rules during this period, allowing fights of varying distances.)[26]

Boxers in Philadelphia contended for "scientific points" and no official decisions were rendered to deter wagering. According to boxing historian Chuck Hasson, "scientific points" reflected the public safety director's vision of how boxing should be conducted in the city. "Of course the people directing the promotions used the term but insinuated to the fighters that they could continue fighting with the same fury that Philly fighters were noted for," said Hasson.[27]

The Quaker City's rabid fight fans weren't dissatisfied with the six-round limit because stalling was not tolerated, and most bouts were fought at a furious pace.

Six-round bouts were also popular with the boxers because they caused less wear and tear than a longer contest, and thus made it easier to fight more often. It wasn't uncommon for boxers of that era to fight twice or more a month.

In the first decade of the 20th century, Philadelphia became the leading site for purse money. Nearly three hundred boxing cards were staged annually in

Philadelphia, with every main event limited to six rounds. Jack Johnson, Sam Langford, Joe Gans, Jack Blackburn, Philadelphia Jack O'Brien, Tommy Ryan, Joe Walcott, Terry McGovern, and other ring greats frequently headlined shows in the city.

What's more, many nationally known boxers who resided in Philadelphia often appeared in six-round main events. Nearly a third of light-heavyweight champion Battling Levinsky's 289 bouts were scheduled for six rounds. Of Jack Blackburn's 172 career bouts 104 were six rounders. (In the 1930s Blackburn gained additional fame as the trainer of legendary heavyweight champion Joe Louis.) Only a fourth of Philadelphia Jack O'Brien's 192 bouts were scheduled for more than six rounds. During New York State's ban on professional boxing (1917–1920) that city's great lightweight champion Benny Leonard often traveled to Philadelphia, where he took on twenty-one opponents in six-round main events.

In 1920 the Philadelphia public safety director raised the maximum fight length to eight rounds within city limits. Two years later, the Pennsylvania legislature—copying New York's example—established a state boxing commission and allowed bouts of up to ten rounds.[28]

The law that prohibited contests beyond six rounds in Philadelphia lasted from 1900 to 1920. Did it make professional boxing safer? During those twenty years, fifteen boxing related deaths took place in Philadelphia. From 1921 to 1941, when the limit was raised to ten rounds, there were only two deaths in Philadelphia rings.[29]

Why would there have been many more deaths before 1921, when six-round bouts were the rule? If shorter fights are safer, shouldn't the opposite have been true? Were boxers throwing caution to the wind in the shorter fights because there was less time to establish dominance? While that is possible, another answer is more probable—the establishment of a state athletic commission in Pennsylvania in 1921, which resulted in stricter regulations and less haphazard medical supervision.

Before 1921 most fights in the state took place with minimum supervision, especially in smaller cities. A lack of basic standards will risk a prizefighter's safety whether the bout is four rounds or twenty rounds. There were often no weigh-ins, no pre-fight medical exams, and few safety precautions. Pennsylvania's new state regulatory agency required that everyone connected with the sport, including referees, be licensed and vetted. As was

A 1903 poster for a typical fight card in Pennsylvania during the six-round era—1900 to 1920. *Author's collection* already the rule in New York, two doctors were required to be at ringside for every fight.

THE CALIFORNIA FOUR-ROUND LAW

From 1901 to 1914 California became a major center for professional boxing as host to more important bouts than any other state. California's boxing laws were less restrictive than those in many other places, and even allowed promoters to determine the number of scheduled rounds. With bare-knuckle "finish fights" not too far in the past, many bouts were scheduled for twenty or twenty-five rounds, and some marathon fights slated for an incredible forty-five rounds. As you might expect, the brutality of some of these early marathon contests caused a backlash. In the November 1914 election, a majority of California voters approved an amendment (known as the "Prize Fights Initiative") that limited bouts to four rounds. Thus began what came to be known as the "Four-Round Era" in California.[30]

Before the law, boxing cards that featured only four-round bouts had been staged in San Francisco with much success and were popular with the fans for several years. The four-round contests generally had a lot more action than longer bouts. Under the new law, boxing arenas throughout California usually featured cards of seven four-round bouts, with the final bout being the most important.[31]

Fighters were content with the new law, as long as they could earn decent paydays. And the law didn't prevent them, of course, from traveling out of state to engage in bouts scheduled beyond four rounds. A typical example is Joe Benjamin, a top lightweight contender in the 1920s, whose ten-year career (1915–1925) coincided with California's four-round law. Fifty-two of his one hundred professional fights were limited to four rounds. His fights went beyond four rounds only when he ventured outside of California.

In 1924, ten years after the four-round law was enacted, California voters approved an amendment that placed professional boxing under the rule of a state athletic commission and also allowed fights of up to ten rounds. As a result, after 1924, cards with only four-round bouts mostly disappeared from the state. By allowing ten-round bouts, California promoters could now stage world title fights that would also result in increased tax revenues for the state. For the next nineteen years, ten rounds remained the limit for both main events and championship fights. It wasn't until 1943 that the first fifteen-round bout was permitted in California.[32]

• • •

Did California's four-round law make boxing safer? The statistics indicate that they did. In the ten years from 1914 to 1924, only one boxing-related death occurred in the state, after a third-round knockout. From November 1924, when longer bouts were allowed, to the end of 1935, by contrast, five deaths occurred, with three of the fatal fights going more than four rounds (KO 10, KO 5, KO 6).[33] Even so, considering the thousands of pro bouts staged in California—at the time it was the busiest boxing state, along with New York—you would have expected the number of ring fatalities to be much higher. I believe the low number is connected to most fights being scheduled for fewer than ten rounds. Ten-round bouts in California were typically confined to experienced professionals. Boxers with fewer than twenty-five fights rarely appeared in a ten-round main event. Instead, boxers still learning their trade typically fought in the six or seven shorter preliminary bouts on the undercard.

POPULARITY UNDIMINISHED

Laws limiting fights to just four or six rounds in California and Philadelphia didn't diminish boxing's popularity. These locations eventually allowed longer fights, but only so they could compete with New York for championship contests.

In 1917—after a boxer was fatally injured in a bout in Albany— reformers convinced the New York state legislature to abolish professional boxing, a ban that lasted three years. After much political maneuvering, professional boxing returned to the Empire State in 1920, after its legislature passed the Walker Law, which allowed title fights scheduled for fifteen rounds.[34] After that, New York quickly reestablished its dominance in the sport.

California, Pennsylvania, and Illinois didn't want to be left out of the bidding for big-money fights and the tax revenues they brought. These states, still unwilling to allow fifteen-round bouts, increased the maximum distance to ten rounds, including for title fights. The ten-round limit did not deter champions from defending their titles in these states, not as long as the money was good. More important, fan enthusiasm for an anticipated championship bout that involved popular boxers didn't diminish if it was scheduled for ten rounds instead of fifteen.

If New York had decided on a ten-round limit in 1920, it would have been accepted everywhere. With only eight weight divisions, and generally one undisputed champion for each, title fights were relatively rare and special events. New York State's increasing "the championship distance" to fifteen rounds was a marketing decision, adding an extra measure of gravitas to championship bouts. Even in New York, though, most nontitle fights remained at the four- to ten-round distances.

THE ST. NICHOLAS ARENA MODEL

Further proof that limiting the number of rounds can improve boxing safety—especially in concert with competent referees and ringside physicians—is revealed in the history of New York City's legendary St. Nicholas Arena. From 1906 to 1962, with a hiatus from May 1917 to September 1920, when the sport was banned in New York State, "St. Nick's" was the busiest boxing arena in the country.[35]

The arena had a four-thousand-seat capacity and showcased some fifteen thousand boxing matches in its long history. (Only one title fight was ever staged at St. Nick's because of its limited seating capacity.) The weekly cards usually consisted of five to seven four-round preliminary bouts and one or two six-round bouts. Sometimes an eight-round semifinal was also included on the undercard. The main event was scheduled for eight or ten rounds. Those numbers suggest that over 80 percent of the approximately fifteen thousand bouts staged at the arena during its fifty-three-year run were scheduled for either four or six rounds. Notably, from 1906 to 1949, no deaths occurred in the St. Nicholas ring.[36]

The first fatalities at St. Nick's occurred in the early television era. In 1950 and 1951, two fighters succumbed to their injuries (KO 10, KO-7). Ten years later, in 1960 and 1961, two more boxers died (KO-10, KO-6).[37] If Patrick Day and Maxim Dadashev, the two ill-fated boxers mentioned in the previous chapter, had been active during the heyday of the St. Nicholas Arena, their limited professional experience would have put them into a six- or eight-round bout.

Today's fighters (and their management) are anxious to engage in televised ten or twelve-round bouts as early in their careers as possible. A victory in a longer bout would indicate they're ready to challenge for an Alphabet title belt and earn larger paydays. It is a dangerous trend, but with so many fabricated

THE FANS OWN RECORD AND OPINION

5c

PROGRAM AND SCORE CARD

Place A Dot . or W in Small Squares ☐ To Indicate Round Boxer Has Won.
A Dash — or L for Lost, X or E for Round Even, S for Stopped, K for Knocked Out.
LF for Lost on Foul, NC for No Contest.

Bout No.	BOXERS TO APPEAR	Aff'n Wght.	Color Trks.	ROUNDS 1 2 3 4 5 6 7 8 9 10	BOXER TO APPEAR	Aff'n Wght.	Color Trks.	Rnds. Schdld.	ROUNDS 1 2 3 4 5 6 7 8 9 10
	Al Reid	129	Blk.		vs. Joey Fontana	133½	Pur.	8	
	Maur. Arnault	137			vs. Victor Troisi	140½		8	
	Bill Pinti	123¾			vs. Nick Lapitino	125½		4	
	Artie Di Pietro	137¾			vs. Tony Gray	134½		4	
	Johnny Craig	130¼			vs. Angelo Lato	146		4	
	Gene Kiernan	129			vs. Angelo DelCanzo	130		4	
	Joe Maldonado	128			vs. John Cockfield	130¾		4	
					vs.				

Monday Eve., October 23rd, 1939

BOXING OFFICIALS

Announcer
Referee
Judge
Judge
Timekeeper

Tel. LOngacre 5-8696

Jap Lord

Custom Made
in our own
workrooms

N. Y. Store
108 West 38th St.
Near Broadway

OFFICIAL DECISIONS

Bout No.	WINNERS	By K.O. Foul Rnd. Min. Sec. By Dec. Rds.	DRAW CONTESTS	LOSERS	Boxers Floored Times Counts
			vs.		
			vs.		
			vs.		
			vs.		
			vs.		
			No Contests		
			vs.		
			vs.		

Tel. Dickens 2-979

Jap Lord
Hatters

Brooklyn Store
1523 Pitkin A
Cor. Saratoga

LOngacre 5-8854

DAVID THOMAS
MEN'S CUSTOM SHOE RETAILERS
$5.85 up

112 W. 38th St. N. Y. CITY

A 1939 program from the historic St. Nicholas Arena (active 1906–1962). Over 80 percent of the arena's fifteen thousand fights were scheduled for between four and six rounds. *Author's collection*

titles and "eliminators" available, hundreds of inexperienced professionals are being rushed into punishing ten- or twelve-round fights.

TAKING A PAGE FROM THE MMA MODEL

Mixed Martial Arts (MMA), a relatively new hybrid combat sport, has become popular in recent years. The sport combines wrestling, boxing, jiu-jitsu, and other fighting disciplines. MMA main events, including title bouts, are limited to five five-minute rounds, with a one-minute rest between rounds. Barring a knockout or submission, the total action time is twenty-five minutes. All other bouts are scheduled for three five-minute rounds, for a total of fifteen minutes. A four, six, or eight-round professional boxing match has twelve to twenty-four minutes of action—if the bouts go the scheduled distance—the same amount of action as MMA bouts.

MMA fans readily accept a bout of three or five rounds (fifteen to twenty-five minutes) because that's the way it has been since the sport's inception, thirty years ago. Perhaps if MMA had started out with ten rounds as the championship distance, there might have been pushback if the bouts were later shortened. But given the sport's history, MMA fans eagerly watch the shorter bouts.

Boxing has been around much longer than MMA and has traditions that go back over one hundred years. Would its fans—who are used to ten- and twelve-round fights—accept five-round main events and eight-round title fights? If history is any indication, I believe they would— just as the fans in California and Philadelphia accepted shorter fights at the turn of the last century.

I am not suggesting that every fight be limited to four or eight rounds. Under the rules I'm advocating, ten-round bouts would be allowed but only if the fighters are sufficiently experienced and evenly matched. There are simply far too many ten- and twelve-round bouts involving combatants who aren't ready for the distance. If a boxing commission with jurisdiction over a bout questions the in-ring history or ability of a fighter, raising the likelihood of a mismatch, it should be scheduled for not more than five rounds. To paraphrase the title of this book, "When in doubt, make it a five-round bout."

• • •

If today's promoters used the St. Nicholas Arena model as their template, the boxers would be vastly safer, and the entertainment quotient wouldn't be affected. Keep in mind that the satisfaction boxing fans—or MMA fans— get from their sport doesn't depend on the number of rounds fought. Boxing fans would rather watch one exciting five- or six-round preliminary bout than two boring twelve-round hugfests. It would make more sense if televised fight cards featured seven or eight preliminary bouts of four-to-eight rounds as appetizers, followed by one or two ten-round main events. Not only would this type of fight card be safer for the fighters, it would also provide a faster-paced show.

ADDRESSING THE OBJECTIONS TO SHORTER FIGHTS

Fans opposed to shortening the fights point to Marciano–Walcott I, Leonard–Hearns I, and Ali–Frazier III as examples of classic bouts that weren't decided until the thirteenth, fourteenth, and fifteenth rounds—the so called championship rounds. But what if these fights had been limited to ten rounds?

How would they be different? Would the results change? Maybe so, but they likely would have been shorter versions of the same fights.

It is also important to note that Marciano, Walcott, Leonard, Hearns, Ali, and Frazier were all experienced professionals, as were their evenly matched top ranked challengers. They were fighting in an era when boxing was still part of mainstream popular culture, when fans had more appreciation for the finer points of boxing technique. This may have resulted from the fact that superior talent was more abundant and on display during network television's Golden Age of boxing, which ended in 1964.

This is the roll call of the ten undisputed world champions that final year: Muhammad Ali (heavyweight); Willie Pastrano (light heavyweight); Joey Giardello (middleweight); Emile Griffith (welterweight); Eddie Perkins (junior welterweight); Carlos Ortiz (lightweight); Flash Elorde (junior lightweight); Vicente Saldivar (featherweight); Eder Jofre (bantamweight); Pone Kingpetch (flyweight). Compare the above list to today's champions in the same weight divisions. If we could time-travel those fighters to the present and have them challenge their counterpart Alphabet champions, what do you think the odds would be? According to most experts, few fighters today come close to matching the seasoned technique and experience of the top fighters of that generation. And for that reason shortening fights wasn't as necessary then as it is now.

• • •

Another criticism: Limiting the number of rounds would eliminate the possibility of a fighter hopelessly behind on points snatching a victory by scoring a sudden knockout in the final moments of a fight scheduled for more than ten rounds. After all, why rob the fighter and the fans of that dramatic possibility? But is it worth the extra risk? You could also argue that the dramatic, come-from-behind knockout would be just as exciting if it came in a final round eight as in a final round fifteen.

Shortening fights would limit exposure to head trauma while not wholly eliminating boxing's excitement and brutality.

• • •

The argument against shorter fights that I find the least convincing is that it's too easy on the fighters, and is comparable to shortening a marathon from twenty-six to thirteen miles. Some fans lament the end of fifteen-round title fights that tested exhausted boxers to the limits of their physical and mental endurance. They argue that being tested this way is what made the winners of these fights so special. How else can you separate the greats from the not so great? Well, if we want to test the limits of fighters' endurance why not really test them and return to twenty-five or forty-five-round contests, or even "finish fights"?

AN EVOLUTIONARY PROPOSAL

While researching and writing this book, as I considered several rule revisions, I found myself wondering whether I had gone too far, or perhaps not far enough, in trying to make the sport safer. Other people have suggested a five-second count out to replace the current ten-second count out; two-minute rounds instead of the current three-minute rounds; a ninety-second break between rounds instead of the current sixty-second break. I do not oppose these well-intentioned changes, but I believe shortening professional fights should take priority over them.

I did not pull this conclusion out of thin air. The statistics compiled over the past forty-three years (see chapter two) reveal that fights scheduled beyond five rounds increase the likelihood of a fatality by up to 70 percent. Limiting the number of rounds won't guarantee a boxer will avoid CTE or that ring fatalities will be eliminated, but it will dramatically lower the frequency of both. A five-round limit for most professional prizefights won't kill the sport—but it will save fighters like Patrick Day, Maxim Dadashev, and Moises Fuentes from *being* killed. It will also eliminate much unnecessary brain trauma. The shorter bouts will also help protect the fighters from poor referees, inadequate ringside physicians, and corrupt or incompetent boxing commissions.

However boxing changes, if it changes at all, I feel a sense of urgency. Lives and brain cells are at risk. Significant changes to boxing's rules of engagement are long overdue.

I realize that a five-round limit may not be an easy sell to the sport's fan base. Is there a compromise that will allow certain fights to be scheduled for more than five rounds while still maintaining a reasonable level of safety? I believe there is, in limited circumstances. Bouts scheduled for ten rounds must be closed to all but the small number of boxers generally recognized as either capable, experienced veterans or elite champions and contenders.

Meanwhile, six- or eight-round bouts must be restricted to evenly matched boxers who may not have yet reached the elite category but are talented prospects with fifty or more pro rounds of experience. If there is any doubt about the ability of one or both boxers, or there are extenuating circumstances—a long layoff or advanced age—the fight must not go beyond five rounds.

But who will decide on the number of rounds? Most state boxing commissions have a medical advisory board. If a boxer fails the commission's medical examination or has been knocked out too many times the board has the authority to suspend his boxing license temporarily or permanently.

In addition to the medical advisory board, every commission should also establish an advisory board capable of carefully reviewing the records and background of each fighter to determine the number of scheduled rounds for the fighter's bouts. If the board finds that the level of experience and skill of two fighters are reasonably matched, then a bout of eight or even ten rounds can be authorized. On the other hand, if the experience and skill level of one or both fighters are unclear—raising the possibility of a mismatch—the board would have the authority to either cancel the bout or limit it to four or five rounds.

Fighters who are disappointed with the advisory board's decision would have the right to petition it for reconsideration. The board's decision must be independent of any aspect of the promotion and be unbiased in its judgment. That would prevent any promoter or sanctioning organization from corruptly influencing the number of rounds in a given fight.

I haven't mentioned twelve-round bouts here because I believe the time has come to eliminate them. Rounds eleven and twelve are unnecessary, especially in today's unsafe environment. As was the practice in California and Illinois for many years, ten rounds should be considered the "championship distance" from now on.

Two recent twelve-round title fights matching elite fighters Terence Crawford against Errol Spence and Tyson Fury against Oleksandr Usyk would have qualified for the ten-round limit. An example of a twelve-round title fight that should never have been allowed to go beyond eight rounds was the September 3, 2024, fight that matched super-bantamweight champion Naoya Inoue against T. J. Doheny in Tokyo. Inoue, a savage puncher, is widely considered the world's best pound-for-pound fighter. Las Vegas oddsmakers made him an overwhelming favorite. Someone betting on Inoue would have had to risk $5,000 to win $100. And the long odds make sense, considering that Doheny at age thirty-seven hadn't beaten a quality opponent in five years.

Not surprisingly, three of the four sanctioning organizations—WBC, IBF, and WBO—approved this horrendous mismatch. For the umpteenth time the opportunity for an Alphabet organization to grab more sanctioning fees took precedence over ring safety.

The result was predictable. It was just a matter of time before Inoue lowered the boom on Doheny. Less than twenty seconds into the seventh round, a solid left hook landed under the challenger's ribs. Doheny turned away in obvious pain, and his right leg buckled. He signaled to the referee that he couldn't continue. He needed assistance to leave the ring. He was lucky— better to be rendered helpless by a body shot than a punch to the head.

The undercard included a twelve-round junior welterweight bout for the WBA Interim title, pitting forty-one-year-old Ismael Barroso against twenty-eight-year-old Andy Hiraoka—another brazen mismatch.

Barroso, the 4-1 underdog, won only one of the first eight rounds on the scorecards. In the ninth round he got knocked down twice, barely beating the count both times. After the second knockdown, Barroso struggled to his feet and looked longingly to his corner. He was silently telling his seconds he was through. But the body language went unnoticed by the referee, who seemed oblivious to what he was looking at. Instead of stopping the fight, he instructed Barroso to take several steps, which the fighter could do. But, as explained in chapters five and six, the fact that a fighter can take a few steady steps after a knockdown isn't a reason to let a one-sided fight continue. Fortunately, before any more damage could be done, Barroso's cornerman, waving a towel, caught the referee's attention and mercifully told him to stop the fight. Once again, boxing's fractured infrastructure and flawed rating system endangered a fighter's life.

Under the more stringent rules suggested in this book the 4-1 odds and Barroso's age would have mandated an eight-round bout. In addition, the referee should have been more aware of the danger to the underdog and been ready to stop the fight sooner rather than later.

Unfortunately, today's fight cards typically feature multiple ten- and twelve-round bouts, regardless of the boxers' experience or skill level. I recently received a press release announcing that two nineteen-year-old bantamweights, twin brothers Ari and Andrey Bonilla, who allegedly had impressive amateur records, would be making their professional debut in

Hollywood, Florida, in ten-round co-main-events. In the entire history of modern boxing, you can count on the fingers of one hand the number of boxers who made their professional debut in a ten-round main event. Even the two Sugar Rays—Robinson and Leonard—both with spectacular amateur records, turned pro in preliminary bouts of four and six rounds, respectively.

• • •

POSTSCRIPT

On February 2, 2024, the same day the manuscript of this book was accepted by the publisher, Japanese bantamweight Kazuki Anaguchi became the first boxing fatality of the year. The twenty-three-year-old had suffered a subdural hematoma in a ten-round fight in Tokyo on December 26, 2023. After emergency brain surgery, he remained in a coma until his death. Anaguchi was a former amateur star but had had only six pro fights (thirty-eight rounds) and had never gone beyond eight rounds. His opponent had eleven fights (sixty-four rounds) and had previously traveled the ten-round distance twice.

Tellingly, Anaguchi managed to outbox his opponent *in the first five rounds*, but after that he began to show signs of fatigue. He then got knocked down three times but lasted the distance and lost a close decision. After leaving the ring, he collapsed in the dressing room.

On paper the fight didn't appear to be a mismatch. The only thing wrong with it was the scheduled distance of ten rounds. If it had been scheduled for five rounds, or even six, instead of ten, a death would likely have been avoided.

In almost a duplicate of Anaguchi's last fight, a second professional boxing-related death took place on July 7, 2024, in Australia. In it Lemuel Silisia (3-0 with 8 rounds of professional experience) lost an eight-round decision to Adam Flood (4-4, 32 rounds). Shortly after the fight, Silisia collapsed. The twenty-seven-year-old was taken off life support a few days later. Considering the fighters' inexperience, this bout should have been limited to four rounds. Silisia reportedly had only one amateur fight before turning pro. Flood had been an Australian Junior amateur champion. But an Alphabet wannabe organization calling itself the World Boxing Foundation advertised the bout for the ersatz "Australasian Super Lightweight title," thereby changing an ordinary preliminary contest into an eight-round main event.

The last professional boxing death of 2024 took place on October 26 in the Pacific Island country of Fiji. The ten-round bout was for the Asia Pacific super featherweight title. The fabricated title was sanctioned by the International Boxing Organization (IBO)—one of about a half dozen minor Alphabet groups looking to grab a piece of the sanctioning-fee gravy train by anointing their own world champions. The bout ended in the ninth round, when Ubayd Haider, 10-1 (51 rounds), was TKO'd by Runqui Zhou, 7-2-1 (73 rounds). The twenty-five-year-old Haider underwent emergency brain surgery and remained in a coma for two weeks before succumbing to his injuries.

Three months later, in Belfast, Ireland, the first boxing death of 2025 saw John Cooney, 11-0 (51 rounds), TKO'd in the ninth round by Nathan Howells, 10-1-1 (65 rounds). The ten-round bout was for the heretofore unknown "British Celtic super-featherweight title." Although no Alphabet organization was involved, the contest was approved by the British Boxing Board of Control (the governing body of professional boxing in the United Kingdom). When the fight was stopped, the ringside television commentator, awed by the amount of head punishment both fighters had absorbed, said they appeared to have "titanium chins." His partner asked if he thought the referee should have called a halt "a bit earlier." The twenty-year-old Cooney passed away one week after undergoing emergency brain surgery. He was one of at least five other professional boxers who had died from fight-related injuries in the previous twelve months.

If the advisory board suggested in this chapter had been in operation, the tragic outcomes could have been averted. None of the aforementioned boxers—based on their limited experience—should have been participating in a bout scheduled for more than four or five rounds. The risks that every boxer takes when he enters the ring are intensified by the stupidity, ignorance, and callousness of the people who organize these travesties. If nothing changes and this trend is allowed to continue, we can expect more of the same.

CHAPTER 4

The Referee's Dilemma

*For the referee, achieving that delicate balance between limiting
punishment and remaining faithful to a sport that demands it
can become a source of unbearable tension.*
—Arthur Mercante Sr.

I don't envy professional boxing referees. They are not simply calling
balls and strikes or fouls and penalties, as in baseball, basketball, or
football. A boxing referee must be prepared to make a split-second
decision to stop a fight. It's a decision that can affect not just a boxer's
career, but his continued existence.

WHEN IN DOUBT, STOP THE BOUT

In a recent interview, an experienced boxing referee said the best referee is one
who neither stops a fight one punch too early nor one punch too late. That
makes superficial sense, but it is virtually impossible to make such a perfect
call every time, or even some of the time. In a real-world boxing match,
it is always better to err on the side of caution and stop a fight one punch too
early rather than one punch too late. Professional boxing would become
immeasurably safer if the following words became every boxing referee's
mantra: *When in doubt, stop the bout.*

To be clear: I'm not trying to rob professional boxing of its intense drama,
nor am I suggesting that a match be stopped as quickly as amateur matches
are. Yes, there have been situations in which a boxer knocked down several

times and—on the brink of defeat—came back and stopped his opponent in a later round. But those are exceptions. If you allow a battered boxer to continue based on the possibility of his turning defeat into victory with a surprise KO, you are gambling with his life, and that's not a risk worth taking.

In a professional boxing match, circumstances can quickly turn bad for one of the fighters. When that happens the referee's training, experience, and instincts are critical, as are his character, courage, and humanity.

When to stop a fight isn't always clear, but mostly it is. Sometimes not stopping a fight soon enough reflects a mistake in judgment. Sometimes it's a lack of training or experience that causes a referee to hesitate at the moment when he should intervene and end the fight. And there may be other, less honorable motives for a referee's failure to stop a fight at the right time.

Professional boxing referees, as we all know, are under pressure to not act too quickly—or too late. They don't want to displease the promoter or the fans, especially in a high-profile fight. Referees know that promoters and the media companies that broadcast fights wield the most power of any actor in the professional boxing industry. Even though the fight takes place within the jurisdiction of a state or country's boxing commission, the promoter usually gets his way when it comes to choosing the referee for a given fight, and referees are fully aware of this.

Understand: referees—and judges—know that if they want to keep working regularly and get the best assignments, they need to be liked by the promoter. When a popular fighter under contract with a major promoter is on the verge of being knocked out, some referees may hesitate to stop the fight even though they know it's the right thing to do. At that point the referee's concern about his own career supersedes the fighter's health and safety.

As for the training and certification of boxing referees, you'd think that a job that involves so much responsibility would require a rigorous training process—but it doesn't. By comparison, the training for referees and umpires in professional football, baseball, and basketball is far more thorough and tightly structured than the training for boxing referees. Umpires in Major League Baseball, for instance, must attend one of two umpiring schools authorized by the League, and it typically takes seven to ten years working in the minors to advance up the ranks to MLB. NBA referees must have had at least two to four years of experience and pass a written exam, and in some cases a floor test, officiating live action. There are similar years-long certification programs for referees in the NFL and NHL that involve advancing through several levels, during which the official's competence is constantly assessed by supervisors.

Professional boxing, unlike the other sports, has no national commissioner or centralized authority to institute a standardized training or certification program. In the United States, each state has its own taxpayer-funded boxing commission, which determines the requirements for a referee's license. Unsurprisingly, these vary from state to state. Elsewhere, licensing requirements vary from country to country, and boxing lacks a standardized training program for referees.

Even more troubling is the lack of oversight. A bad performance by a referee—whether it involves stopping a fight too late or allowing a mismatch to continue round after round—has never been seriously addressed by state or national boxing authorities. In fact, the erring referee is often back working other bouts the following week.

In the absence of a rigorous training program, getting a license to referee professional boxing typically involves observing established referees at work, watching how they maintain control of the bout, how they handle fouls, how they break clinches, and how they handle knockdowns—a process that can take several months. Previous experience working amateur bouts can also help the applicant get a license. In addition, the state or country where referees apply for the license requires them to learn the rules and regulations of professional boxing. Eventually the state or country's boxing commission permits the referee to begin working preliminary matches. If the referee's performance there is considered satisfactory, they move to main bouts.

The novice professional referee quickly realizes that he must abandon habits he may have picked up while officiating three-round amateur contests, in which safety is key and stopping a fight too soon rarely results in criticism. If the newly minted pro referee stops a fight as quickly as he would have stopped a fight in the amateurs, he will be seen as too cautious, and his career in the pros will be short.

● ● ●

Before the 1980s the New York State Athletic Commission didn't announce the names of referees or judges who were slated to work until the night of a fight. This was done to discourage bribes. Nowadays, by contrast, the names of officials are known well beforehand. By pointing this out, I'm not suggesting that today's ring officials are taking bribes, but there are other ways to get to a referee and influence the outcome of a fight. The notorious boxing promoter Don King was known to wine and dine referees and boxing judges who were scheduled to work his shows, which of course involved fighters he controlled. King would also pay their round-trip airfare to wherever a fight was being held and put them up in an expensive hotel—all on his company's tab. The referee and judges knew which fighters King wanted to win. They also knew that if he was dissatisfied with their officiating, it would cost them future lucrative assignments and the perks that went with it.

This soft corruption results in part from the way referees and judges are compensated. In most states their pay scale is set by either the boxing commission or the sanctioning organization whose title is on the line. It is the promoter, however, who is responsible for paying the officials' fees. A referee for a main event or title fight can earn from $2,000 to $25,000, and sometimes much more. Depending on how often the referee works, annual compensation ranges from $40,000 to well over $100,000.[38]

Since the promoter has a financial interest in the fighters headlining his show, any payment he makes to the referee and judges—either directly or indirectly—presents a clear conflict of interest for the person being paid.

● ● ●

A promoter's investment in a specific fighter should never influence a referee's behavior. This would be easier to accomplish if the promoter had no monetary connection to the referee and wasn't involved in referee selection. At present the promoter influences the choice of referee far too much. But there is an easy remedy—referees should be chosen from an independent pool of qualified candidates using a lottery system.

CHAPTER 5
Educating the Referee

erriam-Webster's definition of "concussion": A stunning, damaging, or shattering effect from a hard blow, especially: a jarring injury of the brain resulting in disturbance of cerebral function.

On November 23, 1979, middleweight boxer Willie "Macho" Classen got knocked out by Wilford Scypion in the tenth round of a bout held in the Felt Forum at Madison Square Garden. Five days later, Classen died from a subdural hematoma. Classen's death triggered a state senate investigation that found gross negligence on the part of the New York State Athletic Commission.

The senate investigating committee heard testimony by renowned neuropathologist Bennett Derby M.D., a professor of at the New York University School of Medicine. After viewing a videotape of the bout, Dr. Derby explained that Classen appeared to have suffered a concussion in the round before the round in which he took the knockout punches that eventually killed him. Three consecutive right-hands to the left side of the boxer's head in the ninth round "stopped his clock," Dr. Derby said, and the fight should have been halted then. Instead, the referee let the bout continue.[39]

Classen didn't get any help from the ringside physicians. One of the two doctors assigned to the fight by the New York State Athletic Commission was a pediatrician with no training in trauma or athletic injury and no experience at ringside. This doctor, who was paid fifty dollars for his work that night, testified that he had not even seen the three ninth-round punches; he had been engaged in a conversation and might have been distracted. The other doctor, a urologist, also had no specific training or experience as a ringside physician. Both doctors visited Classen before the start of the tenth round and pronounced him fit to continue.[40]

Within seconds of the bell beginning the tenth round, Classen, who was slow getting out of his corner, took two rights to the head that, in Dr. Derby's view, caused a fatal brain hemorrhage. Dr. Derby explained that it was the fighter's weakened reflexes that left him open to the fatal blows. "In the ninth round I saw exactly when the fight should have been stopped," he testified. "In the tenth round, I saw a man killed in front of my eyes. *All of this was preventable* [emphasis added]."[41]

The New York State Athletic Commission asked Dr. Derby for suggestions to better protect professional boxers. The result was an instructional video conceived and narrated by the doctor and intended for referees and ringside physicians. Though the video was offered to any state boxing commission that requested it, it's not known how many asked to see it.

During my tenure as an inspector with the New York State Athletic Commission (1981–1982) I saw and was impressed by the video. In it Dr. Derby describes an "early warning system" (explained in this chapter) that can help a referee or doctor determine whether a fight should be stopped. I had always assumed that this valuable instructional video would be required viewing for every licensed referee and ringside physician working fights in New York State and perhaps other states as well. I was wrong. As it turned out, few referees or ringside physicians had ever seen the video.

You should never underestimate the potential for bureaucratic incompetence and negligence in a taxpayer-funded organization.

• • •

Let's jump ahead to 2013, shortly after heavyweight boxer Magomed Abdusalamov suffered a severe brain injury in a bout in New York—in the same arena that saw Willie Classen fatally injured—leaving him partially paralyzed and unable to talk. Questions were raised about the medical care that Abdusalamov received from the ringside physicians—even as he exhibited signs of head trauma—as well as about the protocols of the New York State Athletic Commission. In 2017 the severely brain-damaged boxer received $22 million in a settlement with the state of New York.

Six weeks after the bout, I attended a meeting of the Veteran Boxers Association of New York. The guest speaker was the New York State Athletic Commission's medical director, who was one of four doctors on duty the night of the fight. I asked the doctor if he had ever seen the Dr. Derby video. He had no idea what I was talking about. I followed up with a phone call to a deputy commissioner, who also told me he never heard of it. I was told the video had probably been discarded years earlier, during one of the commission's periodic house cleanings.

The loss of this important teaching tool shouldn't have surprised me. There's always a flurry of concern and interest in making the sport safer after a boxer is killed or severely injured in the ring—but that lasts for only a few months. Before long the usual complacency and incompetence sets in, and the commission begins to repeat the mistakes that led to the catastrophe. I'm sure that even before it went missing, the Derby video had been placed on a shelf, gathering dust and forgotten for years. Later generations of referees and ringside physicians never got to see it. Who knows how many boxers could have

Heavyweight Magomed Abdusalamov (right) had emergency brain surgery following his brutal 2013 fight with Mike Perez. New York State paid a record $22 million to settle his lawsuit against the State Athletic Commission. *Getty Images/Photographer: Al Bello*

been saved from unnecessary brain trauma if referees and ringside physicians had the training provided by this video?

Fortunately, several of Dr. Derby's suggestions survived the loss of the video because they were put into effect immediately after the video was made and are still in use (though not consistently) today. These include the "walk to me" command to the fighter following a knockdown, the rule that an ambulance be on standby at the arena, and the requirement of periodic CT scans of a boxer's brain at state expense. Unfortunately, the rest of the doctor's detailed instructions were unavailable once the video disappeared. These included important instruction for referees and ringside physicians on how to recognize and react to the signs of concussion.

After one year as an inspector with the New York State Athletic Commission, I left to become a licensed boxing promoter, prohibited by commission rules from also being an inspector. Before leaving the inspector job, I asked to make an audio recording of Dr. Derby's presentation. The potentially lifesaving information it provides—including the "early warning system"—is still valid today, which is why I have decided to include it in this book.

The following transcription of the audio portion of the video should be required reading for every referee and ringside physician.

• • •

TRANSCRIPTION OF DR. BENNETT DERBY'S LECTURE ON CONCUSSION

"The purpose of this course is to provide the physiological principles on which procedure rests. The decisions are yours. The information permitting you to approach those decisions is what I want to go after right now. This course is for both referees and ringside physicians. It is deliberately constructed in this way because both kinds of people together form a healthcare team."

MINIMIZING THE DAMAGE

"Although the name of the game in other sports is various kinds of contact that may be complicated by concussion and head injury, in boxing it is the total name of the game. The whole point for both boxers is for one participant to produce concussion in the other. This means that you must be prepared to assess the presence of concussion, the length of concussion, how many of them are happening, and most important of all—whether the patient—the boxer—is recovering from the effects of concussion. There is therefore absolutely no thought of preventing concussion. What we wish to do by skillful clinical monitoring is to minimize the chance of tissue damage. Concussion is not necessarily tissue damage but can lead to it. Our job, therefore, is to permit concussion but to minimize the damage. There is, of course, no guarantee that a hard single blow delivered in the right way, in the right time, at the right place can tear a brain apart. But the odds on that are infinitesimal. The usual tissue damage that takes place in boxing is the result of repeated severe blows to the head. If this sequence may be interrupted, tissue damage can be prevented."

RECOGNIZING THE "MINI-CONCUSSION"

"Everybody is familiar with somebody who has seen a match in which there did not seem to be awfully severe concussive head injury occurring, but, yes, a number of mini-concussions occurred only to discover that the boxer doesn't remember the last two rounds. And there's been some clinical research now that's established that such infinitely coordinated activity as playing a violin in a concert can be done with less than complete consciousness. So the simple fact that somebody stands, walks, moves, goes through earlier learned, well-rehearsed movements proves nothing. You must see good muscle tone, sharp performance, good coordination, nice speed, no fall-off in performance. If there is a fall-off in performance, certain abilities are affected, such as seeing an incoming blow quickly and reacting to it quickly and in time. The ability to duck, bob, weave, turn, give with it, stiffen your neck muscles to absorb the impact—all of these things do not work efficiently when you're in a state of partial concussion or recovery from a partial concussion.

"The direct news I'm trying to get across is that a boxer who is in the middle of a mini-concussion is defenseless. Now, he may not be a 'rag doll' down on the floor, but he cannot pick things off that are coming in; and it is this phase, with the inability to protect by stiffening the body, by stiffening the neck and avoidance behavior, where the real brain damage may come. Put another way, a blow that the normal boxer in complete health could handle perfectly capably, under the circumstances I'm describing he may not be able to protect from it capably—and the amount of energy delivered to the head would be more. In that state the boxer is vulnerable to a whole series of punches."

QUESTIONABLE MOTOR PERFORMANCE

"The key linkage between full consciousness and full alertness as observed in the ring (where you cannot exactly sit down and do a lengthy interview) is gauged exclusively from the motor performance of the boxers. So that you look to see if somebody is no longer making nicely coordinated moves, but is merely making simple, stereotyped moves. A great number of the so-called 'slips' that you see may be slips; an equally great number of those are not true slips; they're somebody who for just a split second lost enough consciousness that the tone of their muscles and the coordinative capacity of their legs got interrupted. Instead of there being a complete fall on the floor, there is a momentary slip. In some instances when somebody receives a blow, you can see their knees buckle, just a little bit. This is one of the reasons that it's very important wherever possible to keep boxers off the ropes and out of the corners because this robs you of some of your most key observations. You can see, for example, how if somebody is up against the ropes and has a concussive blow and the knees slump, the boxer does not go on the deck; he is already up against the ropes, and you may or may not be able to be certain what's happening.

"Questionable motor behavior to be aware of includes how the fighters clinch. There is a difference between an observed, goal-directed clinch and somebody who is slumped and is using the other man like a hitching post. It may not last long, but it is one of the signs of a concussion. At such moments the TV ringside commentator will say, 'He's in trouble, he's hurt!' What they are doing is actually describing the effects of a concussion."

LAXITY OF MUSCLE TONE

"Another example of motor enervation is that, although some fighters do not fully close their lips around their mouthpiece, most boxers do. If, after several rounds, the boxer is showing no mouthpiece and then starts to have his lips relax, we are looking at laxity of muscle tone, and this may have meaning. We've all seen a fighter's mouthpiece go flying out of his mouth. That could be the result of a direct blow to the mouth, but usually it means the impact is hard enough to cause a mini-concussion, with a very brief loss of being able to clench the jaw. The relaxation of the lips has allowed slippage of the mouthpiece.

"When a boxer exhibits questionable motor behavior, watch how they dance, watch how they walk. If it's at the end of the round, that's one of the key times to watch. Do they know exactly where the corner is, do they turn to it promptly, and do they walk there in a smart manner. If we could concentrate on the tie-in of motor enervation with consciousness, then we can all come together on what the observations are that we should be making.

"During the fight you have a chance to familiarize yourself with both boxers throughout the entire bout, and you'll be able to see if fatigue is occurring in a gradual or a linear manner, or whether the fatigue seems to be a very new or very abrupt thing. This can be coupled with other observations as to how much riding, coasting, and clinching is occurring.

"A boxer rising from a knockdown must be quickly evaluated by the referee. It is not enough just to observe the boxer standing up, which is very low automatic behavior. A recommendation that you might entertain is under those circumstances make the boxer walk to the referee. Mention one simple little instruction to see what happens.

"So the purpose of this trauma course is not really so much to teach you what concussion is all about—although that's central—it is to get across the vulnerability period of time. The concept of 'micro-concussions' or 'mini-concussions' lasting just a few seconds and with incomplete loss of consciousness is very important because these comprise the overwhelming majority of what will be seen as a hint in terms of the physiological basis for procedure. [In other words, recognizing the physical clues that motivate the referee or doctor to act accordingly.] One might be safe in indicating that the occurrence of a one-second micro-concussion probably is no reason to become excited or alarmed or do anything but note it. Where one draws the line between a half-second micro concussion and a ten-second KO is of course very much a matter of individual clinical judgment on the part of the ringside physician and the referee.

"What I think matters as much as the duration of an individual mini-concussion is how many of them there are in that round, and how many have occurred in the preceding rounds. I think that it's not just the duration of the individual event but whether there's been a series of events. Between rounds you do have the availability to test speech and mental behavior. The first thing that is critical is with every round, no matter what you've seen or not seen, watch that man go back to the corner. You watch that boxer. And you must see for yourself if he knows exactly where to go and goes there. Is he alert or glassy-eyed? Is he slumped all over or is he sitting there with good muscle tone [meaning good posture even while sitting, indicating alertness]. Should there be any question in your mind, you've got sixty seconds to do something about it, and you probably should only take thirty of those seconds. You should ask him simple, oriented questions [as described in the next paragraph]. The fact that the fighter may know his name, place, and time by no means proves that his mental function is normal. If he doesn't know his name, place, and time, right away you're dealing with someone who's had a pretty severe concussion and is not yet recovered from it."

ASKING THE RIGHT QUESTIONS

"Last of all, there is what might be called the integrative, or innovative, or new or non-learned acts. If he's been in this particular boxing arena many times, you don't say, 'Where are you?' He takes one look around and says, 'I'm in a boxing ring.' That is not really the issue. The issue is to ask for new behavior—such as 'How many dimes are there in a dollar?' Or 'Touch your left hand three times against your right knee.' If that direction can be understood quickly and the response correctly carried out quickly, that person, if he had a concussion, has fully recovered from it.

"It should always be kept in mind that the original language goes last and that somebody may be able to respond in Spanish while partly concussed and not be able to speak in English. So if before the fight you know that he has learned English, talk to him in English when you examine him. If you need to talk to him during the fight, you'll immediately discover whether there's been any decay. You need to know the baseline level; this just takes a minute or two visiting the boxer in his dressing room before the fight. Is this a person who always thinks over an answer for two minutes before he answers? There are slow people. I think it's helpful to know not necessarily how many grades of high school the fighter might have had, but certainly in conversation with him to see for yourself how he behaves with simple questions and answers, and that may give you all the information you need at a subsequent time because you have something to compare with."[42]

CHAPTER 6

Modifying the Rules

No referee should take it upon himself to gamble on
a man's recuperative powers.
—A. J. Liebling

THE WEIGH-IN CONTROVERSY

The Association of Ringside Physicians study cited in chapter two included data that showed an increased risk of traumatic brain injury (TBI) in the presence of dehydration (losing water weight), possibly because of a resulting decrease in cerebrospinal fluid. The available evidence suggests that dehydration hurts physical performance in activities involving speed, strength, and endurance. The condition becomes more problematic in the later rounds of a boxing match, as the boxer becomes increasingly fatigued and struggles to block or avoid punches to his head, which he can't absorb as well as in the earlier rounds.[43]

• • •

Before the 1980s, boxers usually weighed in between 10 A.M. and noon on the day of the fight, as was the custom going back to bare-knuckle days. That changed, however, in the early 1980s, when boxing commissions decided to make boxers weigh in at least twenty-four hours before the fight. The change was said to be for safety reasons. Specifically, the day before early weigh-ins would give boxers who struggled to make weight time to rehydrate.

Actually safety had little to do with getting rid of same day weigh-ins. The real motivation was economic. In 1983, Eddie Mustafa Muhammad came in overweight for a light-heavyweight unification match with Michael Spinks. This highly anticipated title fight was to be televised by HBO. At the weigh-in, which took place, as usual, on the day of the fight, Mustafa weighed in at 180 pounds—five pounds over the contracted weight limit. When he proposed that the fifteen-round title fight be changed to a ten-round nontitle fight, Spinks told him where to go. Spinks refused to go forward with the fight because he'd sacrificed and trained hard and lost the weight and felt his opponent should have, too. The fight's cancellation was a major embarrassment for HBO and the promoters, who were left holding the bag.

To avoid the situation's ever happening again, the promoters, television networks, and the Alphabets agreed to switch all weigh-ins to the day before the fight. All three put a positive spin on the change by pretending it was for the "health" and "security" of the fighters.

Those who opposed starting weigh-ins twenty-four or more hours before the fight included many old-school trainers. They argued that the early weigh-in would encourage a fighter having trouble making weight to starve himself to make weight and then rehydrate over the next twenty-four hours, during which time the fighter could gain back twelve to twenty pounds. But a dehydrated fighter can't rehydrate by drinking large amounts of water in the twenty-four hours leading up to a fight—it takes several days for the musculoskeletal system to rehydrate and recover. As for the brain, it isn't known how long it takes for it to rehydrate.

No matter whether the weigh-in takes place on the day of the fight or the day before, it is never a good idea for a boxer to go into a fight dehydrated. The danger of dehydration is this: it diminishes the protective cerebrospinal fluid that surrounds the brain and fills in the spaces between its cells. And a brain that is short of cerebrospinal fluid takes longer to recover from the shock of a punch, increasing the severity of the damage suffered.[44]

It is difficult to know whether dehydration's effect on the brain can contribute to a boxing fatality. Perhaps the fatality resulted instead from weakness and a lack of stamina that made it harder for the dehydrated fighter to defend himself in the later rounds.

Lighter-weight boxers—from flyweight to lightweight—tend to cut a higher percentage of body weight before weigh-ins, which can place them at a higher risk for a TBI. Dehydration could also explain why fatalities frequently occur later in the bout, when it increases. The danger grows exponentially with mismatched boxers, boxers who have poor defensive skills, and incompetent or negligent referees and physicians.

The early-versus-same-day-weigh-in debate rages on, with advocates on both sides. Dr. Flip Homansky, the former medical director of the Nevada State Athletic Commission, favors going back to same-day weigh-ins: "If the boxers fought in the right weight class for their body size, it wouldn't matter. The weigh-in could be anytime. . . . Going back to the morning of the fight would be more uniform. It would decrease abuse. A welterweight should go into the ring weighing not much more than 147; it is a crime when a kid weighing almost 160 fights someone weighing 149."[45] Homansky is right. A boxer fighting at his natural weight does not have to dehydrate. Even if forced to weigh in twenty-four hours before the fight, he would not have to rehydrate, and on the night of the fight he would remain within a pound or two of his natural weight.

Given its dangers, state boxing commissions should require boxers and trainers to take a mandatory seminar on dehydration and why boxers need to fight at their natural weight.

THE STANDING EIGHT COUNT: YEA OR NAY?

As noted in chapter five, a referee should always be alert to changes in the boxer's motor coordination. Both the referee and the ringside physician must be aware that when a boxer slumps or staggers after taking a punch—even for a second or two—that is the sign of a mini-concussion. In a mini-concussion the boxer is knocked briefly unconscious and cannot defend against follow-up punches. There's also a concurrent loss of tension in the neck muscles—as they temporarily relax—during which a follow-up punch will cause the head to snap violently, and the brain to slam with greater than normal velocity against the inside of the skull. To prevent that from happening and give the fighter a chance to regain his bearings, the rules should allow the referee to immediately stop the action and administer a "standing eight count," after which he can determine the fighter's condition before the fighter gets hit with another punch.

At the completion of the eight count, the referee will take several steps back and tell the fighter to "walk to me." He will then tell him to "step to the side." Any unsteadiness—at either command—indicates to the referee that he must stop the fight and award victory to the opponent. If the fighter has obeyed the referee's commands without stumbling, the referee will let the fight continue, with one point deducted from the fighter's score, since the standing eight count is scored as a knockdown. Three standing-eight counts to the same fighter in the same round will automatically end the fight and result in a TKO (technical knockout) victory for his opponent.

The standing eight count is not the same as a "mandatory eight count," which occurs when a fighter is knocked down and the referee counts off eight seconds no matter how quickly the fighter gets to his feet. Standard in all amateur bouts, the standing eight count is not currently used in professional boxing, but it should be.

There are dozens of videos of fights on YouTube with segments where a standing eight count would have been appropriate—if the referee had had that option. The May 13, 2023, WBO middleweight title bout between Zhanibek Alimkhanuly and Steven Butler is a textbook example. In the second round, a punch staggered Butler, leaving him virtually helpless, unsteady, and unable to defend himself. This would have been the perfect time for the referee to call for a standing eight count. Two brutal knockdowns quickly followed the blow. It was obvious to the ringside TV commentators and everyone in the audience—but apparently not the referee—that the fight should have been stopped. After Butler was knocked down for a third time, at which point the referee finally stopped the fight. I don't know if it was incompetence or a fear of stopping the fight too soon, but this referee, with over twenty years of experience, should have known better.

I do not wish to single out any particular referee because so many referees are guilty of the same behavior. But without a system to discipline referees for anything from incompetence to a temporary lapse in judgment, referees will continue to endanger fighters.

• • •

The first Tyson Fury–Oleksandr Usyk heavyweight title fight is another bout that called for a standing-eight count. With less than a minute to go in round nine, Fury was staggered by Usyk's left cross to his jaw. Fury's body slumped momentarily—the perfect time to call a standing eight count—and for the next twenty seconds, he stumbled around the ring on unsteady legs. Usyk landed several follow-up punches that kept Fury floundering, clearly in trouble.

At least three times during the ninth round, a standing eight would have been appropriate to assess Fury's condition. But since there was no standing eight count rule in effect, the referee had no choice but to choose between stopping the fight or letting it continue. One could sense the conflict in the referee's mind as he watched Fury staggering from one side of the ring to the other. Near the end of the round, yet another punch from Usyk caused Fury to fall back against the ropes. It was at this point that the referee, obviously relieved, called the first knockdown. (The rules state that if the ropes prevent a fighter from falling, it counts as a knockdown.) The round ended a few seconds after the referee completed the eight count. The fact that Fury could continue to fight (he lost the twelve-round decision) is beside the point. *When in doubt, stop the bout.*

● ● ●

As was the case in Fury–Usyk I, a hurt boxer will often retreat to the ropes while trying to defend himself. A referee must be aware that when a fighter is supported by the ropes or trapped in a corner, it is difficult to accurately gauge his motor coordination. Deciding when to call a standing eight count may not be as easy. The noted referee Arthur Mercante Sr. considered a boxer trapped against the ropes or in a corner to be in a dangerous situation. He made sure to position himself close to the fighters in case it became necessary to quickly stop the fight.

Every referee should view the YouTube video of Ray Mercer's brutal knockout of Tommy Morrison to see why it is so important for the referee to be in the right position to stop the fight or call a standing eight count when a fighter is trapped on the ropes. During Mercer's assault, Morrison was unconscious for several seconds, but the ropes kept him from falling. Mercer had landed several solid punches to his helpless opponent's head before the referee belatedly intervened. Instead of moving to the side of the fighters when Morrison was backed up to the ropes, the referee stayed several feet behind Mercer and thus was in a poor position to know if it was time to stop the fight.

Because the standing eight count allows the referee to evaluate the fighter's physical and mental condition at a crucial moment, I believe most referees would welcome it. Even if a fighter does not show signs of a mini-concussion, a standing eight count may still be appropriate. There are fighters who can absorb head punches round after round yet show no outward indication of

Ray Mercer about to hit an unconscious Tommy Morrison, whose body is supported by the ropes. *Getty Images/The Ring Magazine Collection*

distress. Nevertheless, they may still be suffering serious brain trauma. The more hits to the head, the more cumulative damage to the brain. A standing eight count is especially appropriate for this type of fighter. It not only gives the referee a chance to evaluate his condition but also serves as a warning that if he continues to take too many punches, the fight will be stopped.

The option to use a standing eight count would also benefit those referees who hold off on stopping a fight to give the hurt fighter every chance to come back. As one referee put it, "I like to see a definitive ending." This is both wrong and dangerous.

Critics of the standing eight count say it gives the hurt fighter a chance to recover, which exposes him to even more punishment if the bout is then allowed to continue. According to this argument, if the boxer is hurt enough to call a standing eight count why not just stop the fight? That makes sense in some cases, but it misses the purpose of the standing eight count, which is to interrupt a potentially dangerous sequence of follow-up punches to a momentarily defenseless fighter who's experiencing a mini-concussion.

Can we be sure of the rule's effectiveness every time? Of course not. There is always the chance that some referees will call a standing eight count when it's not necessary. But it gives a hesitant referee extra time to decide whether or not to stop the fight. Without the option to call a standing eight count, the referee may decide to let a bout continue and wait for the hurt fighter to take another series of unanswered punches, or a knockdown or two, before being convinced to end it. The result of that behavior is additional punishment, or worse, for the fighter.

Another criticism of the standing eight count is that it interrupts the natural ebb and flow of the fight. Many fans consider it unfair to the other fighter, who might have won by knockout had his attack not been interrupted. I believe this is the reason why several states that had the standing eight count in their rule books have since discontinued its use. But if interrupting the ebb and flow of a fight is the cost of saving a boxer from unnecessary punishment, I'm OK with that. These criticisms are, in my opinion, not strong enough to overcome the safety benefits of the standing eight count.

If referees always stopped fights at exactly the right time—neither one punch too early, nor one punch too late—which is of course impossible, boxing wouldn't need a standing eight count rule. To those opposed to it, I say why not enact the rule on an experimental basis for one year. That would expose its weaknesses and strengths and give us a better handle on whether it should be made permanent.

WHAT THE UFC CAN TEACH US

It is instructive to note that since its inception, in 1993, there hasn't been a single fatality in the Ultimate Fighting Championship (UFC), the largest MMA promotion company, which is not the case in other, less-regulated MMA organizations. From April 2019 to July 2023, there have been seven recorded deaths that resulted from sanctioned MMA contests and at least nine from unregulated MMA bouts.[46] Perhaps that's because the UFC suspends referees who tend to stop fights too late. Professional boxing cannot rely on promoters or sanctioning organizations to do the same. That's another reason why, in the interest of safety, state athletic commissions should establish an independent peer-review committee to critique a referee's performance after every fight. It is the only way to weed out referees who continually let fights go on too long.

TAKING A KNEE

On July 15, 2023, in Las Vegas, Nevada, lightweight boxer Frank Martin (17-0) won a close twelve-round decision over Artem Harutyunan (12-0) in a fight broadcast by Showtime. Even though no title was at stake, the promoters wanted to add some gravitas to the fight, so, with the approval of the Nevada State Athletic Commission, it was scheduled for twelve rounds.

Martin was coming on strong in the final three rounds. Harutyunan's eye was swollen shut, and he was having trouble evading his surging opponent's punches. Much like a basketball player who calls time out to interrupt an opposing team's momentum, Harutyunan wisely decided to initiate his own time out by taking a knee. The referee correctly ruled this a knockdown. Harutyunan got up before being counted out, finishing the round but losing the decision.

One rarely sees a boxer "take a knee," and I doubt we will ever see much of it, but it could function as an additional safety net. It may have to overcome some resistance from the fans, however. Many fans who are drawn to boxing's violence don't really care about the technical aspects of the "noble art of self-defense," especially the defense part. They certainly don't want to see a boxer killed or severely injured, but they expect and want to see knockouts—and the more brutal, the better.

But no athletic event is more important than a person's life. Fighters should be encouraged to take a knee if on the receiving end of a damaging barrage of punches. The rules allow for it, but many fighters don't even know they have the option. For that reason, it should be part of the referee's instructions to the fighters before every bout.

If a fighter who takes a knee gets up before being counted out, the referee should ask if he wants to continue. Taking a knee could indicate that the fighter is looking for a way out, and the question will give him the opportunity to call it a night. If the fighter gives an oral "yes," then the referee should follow the same procedure as he would follow after a regular knockdown, asking the fighter to step forward and to the side before deciding whether the bout should continue.

To make sure the rule is not abused, a fighter should only be allowed two opportunities to take a knee without forfeiting the bout. If he takes a knee a third time, the referee will stop the fight and award victory to the opponent. It will go into the record books as a TKO.

Most boxers will avoid taking a knee voluntarily. They feel compelled to live up to the warrior's code. So it's up to referees—and ringside physicians—to save the boxers from themselves. But the fighter who chooses to take a knee a third time (which automatically ends the fight) should not be criticized or vilified for deciding he's had enough. It is galling when some TV announcers, sitting safely at ringside, denounce a fighter for quitting. It is the fighter, not the critics, who must live with the damaging consequences of his profession.

THROWING IN THE TOWEL

Throwing a towel into the ring to save a fighter from further punishment is an antiquated but effective signal of surrender. In Europe, the rules still allow it. The same is true in California, the busiest boxing state. But in Nevada it isn't allowed. There the weakened fighter's chief second must first notify the inspector that he wants the fight stopped; the inspector then climbs up to the ring apron and signals to the referee that the corner wants to stop the fight. New York also doesn't allow a towel to be tossed into the ring. The chief second must first notify the ringside doctor he wants the fight stopped. The doctor then signals the referee to end it.

The Nevada and New York rules waste precious seconds during which the fighter will likely suffer further unnecessary punishment.

Perhaps with this in mind, the New York State Athletic Commission, as of September 2024, has tried to speed the process up by allowing the doctor to use an air horn to signal the referee to quickly stop the fight. The air horn can be used anytime the doctor feels the fight should be stopped, including when the doctor has been asked to stop the fight by the fighter's chief second. Still, why bother with an extra step? What's wrong with just throwing in the towel without involving middlemen? And let's make the procedure universal. The boxer's chief second—usually the fighter's trainer—often recognizes that his fighter is in danger of serious harm before the referee or doctor does, and therefore the chief second should be allowed to end the fight by throwing a towel into the ring.

Another way to stop a fight is for a cornerman to climb into the ring during the round, which will end the fight by getting his fighter disqualified. However, throwing a towel into the ring works even faster. If the referee doesn't see the towel right away—the timekeeper, upon seeing it, should ring the bell as a signal for the referee to act. A fight ending this way would go into the record books as a TKO (loss by technical knockout).

MOUTHPIECE INTERRUPTUS

A boxer's mouthpiece is custom made by a dentist from a rubber-like material. It protects the teeth and is believed to absorb some of the energy of a punch.

It is difficult to dislodge a properly fitted mouthpiece, but it does happen occasionally. Before the 1980s the rules didn't allow the action to be interrupted when a boxer lost his mouthpiece by accident. Instead, the referee would wait for a lull in the action, at which point he would retrieve the mouthpiece from the floor and toss it toward the fighter's corner. The cornerman would then have the mouthpiece washed off and ready for when the round ended and the fighter returned to his corner.

Today's rule calls for the referee to halt the fight during a lull in the action, pick up the mouthpiece, and walk the fighter back to his corner, where a cornerman quickly washes and returns it. All this is done for the fighter's protection, but not everyone is happy with the interruption to the normal ebb and flow of the bout.

What happens when a fighter takes advantage of the rule and deliberately spits out his mouthpiece to interrupt his opponent's attack? Under present rules that is handled the same way as if he had accidentally lost the mouthpiece, although the referee will issue a warning to the fighter. There may be a point deduction, but that, too, is up to the referee. A new rule should require the referee to call a halt and administer a standing eight count. In other words, deliberately spitting out the mouthpiece would be handled the same as if the fighter had taken a knee. If the fighter deliberately spits out his mouthpiece *a second time*, either in the same round or in a subsequent round, the fighter should automatically be disqualified.

One refinement to my proposed rule: Spitting out one's mouthpiece after being knocked down should be considered the same as surrendering, and cause an automatic disqualification—not a simple point deduction. Such a rule should have been enacted after the 2005 lightweight title fight between Diego Corrales and Jose Luis Castillo, in Las Vegas, Nevada, which ended with a tenth-round TKO victory for Corrales.

While I have always viewed the ending of that fight as terribly flawed, many fans celebrate the fight because of Corrales's dramatic comeback. (After suffering two hard knockdowns, he then stopped Castillo in the same round.) But Corrales should have been disqualified because after each knockdown he deliberately spit out his mouthpiece to gain extra time to recover.

Corrales barely beat the count both times. But instead of disqualifying him, the referee stopped the action after each knockdown to retrieve the mouthpiece. When Corrales got up, the referee walked him back to his corner, where his manager rinsed the mouthpiece and placed it back in his mouth.

The referee wasted even more time by delaying the action after the second knockdown, to tell the judges to deduct one point from Corrales's score for spitting out the mouthpiece. Once again, he took Corrales back to the corner to replace the mouthpiece a second time. In all, not including the nine-count knockdowns, Corrales was given twenty-nine extra seconds to recover.

What must Castillo have been thinking while this was happening? He had done everything necessary to secure a victory in a brutal and hard-fought contest. But he couldn't overcome his combined exhaustion and frustration, as well as an inappropriate rule. Given extra and unwarranted time to recover, Corrales came back with a desperate Hail Mary left hook that sent Castillo into the ropes. Castillo didn't go down, but he was near collapse when the referee intervened to stop the fight. Corrales should have given his championship belt to the referee for helping him unfairly turn defeat into undeserved victory.

In the long run the referee didn't do Corrales any favors, though. He was never the same after the beating he took, and he lost his next three fights, including a fourth-round knockout to Castillo in their rematch.

CHAPTER 7

A Referee Speaks
Out—Anonymously

On the condition that he remains anonymous, a professional boxing referee agreed to be interviewed for this book. I have watched this referee work many times and chose to interview him because of his years of experience and competence.

MS: How does one prepare or learn to become a professional boxing referee?

REF: Everyone's path is a little different. Usually, you start out working in the amateurs. Hopefully you have good mentors and a trainer who can help you hone your skills. After getting some experience—and the type of experience one gets can vary greatly—you can then apply to get your professional referee license from your state or country's boxing commission.

MS: What advice would you give a beginner referee?

REF: I would first ask the beginner referee, "Why do you want to be a referee?" But before you answer, ask **yourself,** why do I want to be a referee? Then truly and honestly look into your soul and check your motives before you answer. If you want to be a referee for the wrong reason, then don't do it. Refereeing boxing is not a game. It can be life or death, and will you be able to handle that? Second, find a good mentor/trainer—someone you can trust and has your best interest at heart.

MS: That is great advice. What do you see as the most important quality of a good referee?

REF: The most important quality is knowing when to stop a fight. Any referee who says anything different is not qualified to be a referee. Know what is happening in front of you. Exceptional judgment is required. Knowing when a fighter still has a chance to win the fight, or is it time to stop [the fight]? An understanding of ring mechanics, movement and positioning; knowing when to step in close or close the gap, and when to stay out of the way; knowledge of the rules, and how and when to apply them. Ring generalship; control of self, fighters, corners. Compassion for the fighters. Courage and a thick skin. Willingness to learn and improve.

MS: What should a referee look for when deciding to stop a fight?

REF: Can the hurt fighter defend himself? Does the fighter still have what it takes to win? Is the fighter trying to win or just survive? Watch body language. Observe the gait as he walks back to his corner and sits down. Note the communication with his cornermen. Is he listening? Is he comprehending? Or is he just in outer space? Observe the fighter's breathing pattern and muscle tone. Are his punches missing the mark by a wide margin? How many clean power shots has the fighter taken?

MS: Obviously you have to be laser-focused on the fighters.

REF: All these little clues begin to build up in my mind. You may need to start standing a little bit close and look into the fighter's eyes. Let's say it's the tenth round of a twelve-round fight. A referee is not supposed to look at the scorecards, but in my mind the fighter has lost most of the previous rounds. Does he still have it in him to win the fight? At this point he can only win by a knockout. But does he have the power to knock out his opponent? If in my opinion he does not, and there is no way for him to win the fight, why am I going to let him take a beating for another two or three rounds when I know in my heart there's probably no way in hell this guy is going to win this fight? Then I would have to stop the fight.

MS: You've refereed all over the world. Who decides if you or someone else will referee a particular fight?

REF: There is no set pattern as to who gets chosen to referee. A lot depends on who's at the helm making the calls. In the US it varies from state to state. You may have a very strong state boxing commission, such as in Nevada, and they will basically say to the promoter and sanctioning organization, "These are the refs we're going to use, and these are the judges we're going to use." Some state boxing commissions will not be intimidated by a promoter or sanctioning body, but then you have others that are maybe not as strong and maybe not as knowledgeable. If you have a commissioner who is not strong, or is incompetent, or lacks judgment, he (or she) may agree to their demands. The promoter or sanctioning organization can call and say, "Listen, we don't want to use your referee, but if you play ball with us we'll come back and do another show in your city," that kind of thing. So they give them what they want.

MS: What is the role of the sanctioning organization in relation to who gets chosen to referee?

REF: In addition to obtaining a license in his home state, a referee must join a sanctioning organization if he wants to be put on their list of recommended referees. If you want to work a title fight sanctioned by the WBC, WBA, IBF, or WBO, you must pay a membership fee and attend their annual conventions.

MS: So if a referee wants to be considered for a title fight, or some other high-profile fight, it's not enough just to be licensed in his home state? He also has to join the sanctioning organizations that are private for-profit entities with no legal power other than the authority voluntarily granted to them by boxing commissions?

REF: Yes. You have to pay annual membership fees and attend their conventions and seminars that also involve spending thousands of dollars for hotels and airfare. Without doing this you will never be recommended by them. But it doesn't matter which organizations you belong to; there is no guarantee that you'll ever get work. The WBC is the worst because they don't want you working with any other organization. If you accept a refereeing assignment from another organization, you will never get assigned to work another WBC fight. It's an unwritten rule, but everyone knows it. To the WBC it's like you're being disloyal. They want you to be a WBC referee and only referee WBC sanctioned fights.

MS: Are you saying that a qualified referee will be prevented from working a WBC fight just because he accepted an assignment for a fight sanctioned by a rival organization?

REF: Let's say you are also with the WBO or the IBF and they assign you to a fight outside of the United States. If the WBC finds out about it, guess what? You get no more work from the WBC in South America, Mexico, England, or wherever. Even if you remain loyal to the WBC, if you make what they consider to be a wrong call while working one of their fights, they can decide to ice you.

MS: Can you give an example?

REF: Let's use for an example the close relationship between Don King and the WBC. King may have a bunch of champions and contenders in the WBC ranking system. Let's say I make a call during a King-promoted title fight and he didn't like my officiating because it appeared to King that I didn't favor his fighter. Maybe I ruled a knockdown that he thought wasn't a knockdown, or he might question my judgment in stopping the fight. King could call up the WBC and say, "I don't want that referee to work any more of my fights. If any of my guys are fighting for a WBC title, I do not want him as a referee." So what happens? When a WBC title fight comes up in the future, I won't get the assignment. The sanctioning organizations aren't going to tell you why they won't use you on a Don King or a Bob Arum show or whoever; they're just going to freeze you out of future assignments.

MS: Does the referee have any recourse in that situation? What about the state or country's boxing commission where the fight is taking place? Don't they have a say as to who is assigned to referee a fight?

REF: In the US, the state boxing commission where the fight takes place will announce the names of the referee and judges who will officiate. It is possible that you could have a strong state boxing commission that says, "We won't honor [the promoter's] request to assign another referee because as far as we're concerned, he's a good referee and we're still going to use him." That commission is going to do what is best for boxing, not necessarily what's best for the promoter or sanctioning organization, even if the promoter threatens to move his show to a more accommodating state. In Europe and South America, most boxing commissions give in to the promoter or sanctioning organization and allow them to choose who will referee and judge the fights. There is a lot of stuff that evolves behind the scenes, a lot of politicking, and a lot of power-playing going on. It's unfortunate because, again, it depends on the state or country's boxing commission to stand up to the promoter and sanctioning organization and not let them influence who will referee or judge the fight.

MS: What would happen if a referee made it clear to the sanctioning organizations and promoters that he could be relied on to be totally fair and impartial when officiating and would never favor one fighter over another?

REF: I know for a fact that someone from the WBC approached a referee before a title fight and said if this or that happens, we want this to happen. He was basically telling the referee he wanted a particular fighter to win. And the referee said, "I'm not going to do that. I don't play favorites, that's not the way I am," and after that he was done with the WBC. They never assigned him to another fight.

MS: Do the sanctioning organizations have a rating system for their referees?

REF: No. They do not rate their referees on quality. For the WBC all that matters is that you are loyal to the WBC, no matter if you suck as a referee. They would rather keep a mediocre but loyal referee working than assign a better referee from a rival sanctioning organization.

MS: Wouldn't that risk the safety of the boxers?

REF: Of course. If the WBC won't use you because you are a member of a rival sanctioning organization, they are not hurting themselves. They are hurting the fighter because they are getting a subpar referee. Fighters deserve the best possible referee and judges that they can get.

MS: What can be done to change the present system?

REF: If you are a certified, state-licensed referee, you should not have to join any sanctioning organization. In fact, it should be considered a plus not to join. The boxing commission where the fight is taking place should be able to say, "We want the best, and we think this guy is the best, even if he's not a member of the WBC and hasn't attended any of their conventions." Referees and judges should be totally independent of any sanctioning organization because those groups are tight with the promoters, who endorse certain fighters. The referee's sole purpose is to protect boxers and see that rules are followed. There is no reason for a licensed referee to have to align with any sanctioning organization. The WBC, WBA, IBF, and WBO should have absolutely no say in who referees or judges.

MS: Knowing that the sanctioning organizations and the promoter have so much influence on who gets assigned must put a lot of pressure on referees who are chosen to work a fight.

REF: The bigger the fight, the more you're going to be under the microscope. I have seen a lot of referees not handle the pressure well. They fear the consequences of not pleasing the promoter, the sanctioning organizations, or the fans. They'll say to themselves, "I'm not going to get another fight . . . this promoter is trying to blackball me . . . the fans are going to get on me . . . I'm going to be crucified by the media . . . I'd rather let the fighter get knocked out." That mindset often results in the referee waiting too long to stop the fight.

MS: How do you handle that type of pressure?

REF: I never let anything influence how I handle a fight—not the crowd, not the corners, not the fighters, not the promoter, not the manager, not the media. I'm OK with that because at the end of the day, I can go to bed with a clear conscience, knowing that I did the best possible job. The bottom line is that if you have someone with the courage and character, they will stand up to the heat; because the heat's going to come, there's no doubt about it. You've got to have the courage to do what you need to do. Whether it's a four-rounder or a twelve-rounder, I'm there for the fighters. I'm going to referee the same way because each of those fighters deserves the best possible referee. That's it. I don't care. But very seldom will you find a referee with that kind of mentality.

MS: Has staying true to your principles affected your getting referee assignments?

REF: Probably. But it's hard to say, as I don't know what goes on behind closed doors. There could be other factors involved. Did a promoter get to a state's boxing commissioner and complain that I stop fights too soon? Or maybe the commissioner and I don't see eye to eye? You never know.

MS: Would boxing be better off if it had only one sanctioning organization as opposed to four?

REF: Yes. There should be one honest sanctioning organization. But it will never happen.

MS: What would you like to see happen?

REF: The WBC must not be allowed to blackball referees just because they belong to another organization. Boxing referees should form a union, like in the NHL, NBA, NFL, and Major League Baseball umpires and refs. New referees coming up must be trained better than the old ones. All of the referees in other professional sports undergo standardized training protocols, and they are always getting evaluated. Assignments to championship tournaments go to the best referees. You know that if you've made it to that level, you're going to be working a certain amount of games. You're all under the same umbrella. It's not politics or who you are related to. There are no sanctioning bodies to get involved with. Boxing could work the same way, so you know you're getting the cream-of-the-crop of referees. It's not right that the boxing promoter should control who is assigned as a referee or judge. Under the current system it's like the Yankees are playing a home game and the owner of the team insists that only Yankee fans living in New York can be the umpires.

MS: What else would you change?

REF: Boxers should be encouraged to fight at their natural weight. It is safer than overtraining or starving yourself to make weight and come in dehydrated, which is extremely dangerous.

MS: How important is the physical condition of the referee?

REF: Like a fighter, a referee can get ring rust. There are some guys out there still refereeing who should be retired. They should not be working as referees. But they still are, and it's a shame because the fighter is the one who pays the price. I try to be in the best possible shape when I referee. I would never jeopardize a fighter's health. I've taken myself out of a couple of fights because of an injury or this or that, and people say, "Oh you could still referee." But I'm not going to put somebody in jeopardy because I'm not well.

MS: Do you think there should be better training for referees and more seminars that educate them in knowing the signs of when to stop a fight?

REF: Absolutely. One of the things that really bothers me is to hear a referee say he prefers to let the fight take its natural course: "If the guy gets knocked out, then he gets knocked out." You're saying this while the fighter could be dying on the ropes. You have no compassion for this guy. You've got to save the guy's life. This is a culture and mindset that needs to change.

CHAPTER 8

Hands Up, Chin Down: Reviving a Lost Art

The idea of boxing is to hit and not get hit. You should tell your
boxers never to forget that for a moment. Boxing is all about balance.
It is stupid to stand and trade punch for punch like you see lots of
these kids doing today on television. There's no sense in that.
I know the sluggers and the big punchers are the darlings of the
television audiences, but there is no skill or longevity in doing that.
—Willie Pep, featherweight champion of the world 1942–1948,
1949–1951. Final record: 229-11-1

B oxing skill should be part of the conversation, as a way to make
the sport less dangerous.

Over the past quarter century, boxing skills have deteriorated
significantly, especially when it comes to defense. Boxers are
getting hit way too often, with punches they could have avoided if they prac-
ticed the lost arts of blocking, ducking, parrying, slipping, side-stepping,
weaving, and rolling. These techniques—used routinely by champions and
contenders of decades past—are no longer taught or encouraged. Today's
focus is on aggression and trying to overwhelm your opponent with power
punches. When boxing technique is absent, physicality determines the winner. The fighter who is stronger, faster, and can take a better punch will
typically win.

Few boxers today use mobile footwork, a key part of an effective defense.
Instead, to generate extra power, fighters spread their legs too far apart,

Peerless featherweight champion Willie Pep jabs Chalky Wright in their 1942 title fight. *Author's collection*

limiting their movement. Most of today's fighters, from flyweights to heavyweights, shuffle forward or back in a straight line—instead of presenting an elusive target by quickly moving left or right after getting off a volley. Instead, they remain stationary and become an easy target for a counterattack. Today's most common defensive maneuver is this: a fighter holds his gloves in front of his face and waits for his opponent to stop punching before he resumes his own attack. Gone is the art of slipping or parrying an opponent's punches and countering with combinations. Today's fighters also don't seem to gauge distance properly or step in with their jab. It's a rare treat to see a fighter execute an old-school feint or draw a lead to set up an opening. The same is true for effective body punching and the lost art of infighting.

Granted, these techniques aren't easy to learn. The boxer must be shown how to execute them, and even then it can take three to five years before these skills develop. But without good teachers and the time and experience it takes to master these skills, progress remains limited.

But even basic strategies are not being taught. For example, boxers used to go instantly from offense to defense and vice versa because that's how they

Today's most used defensive strategy: Placing gloves in front of the face while waiting for the opponent to stop punching. *Showtime*

were taught and developed. Today's boxers are taught to do these things separately. If they go on offense, they lose their defense. If they go on defense, their offense freezes.

Many past contenders and champions weren't truly great boxers, but they were *highly skilled* boxers—much too skilled, experienced, and savvy for today's contenders and champions.

The 1920s to the 1950s was a Golden Age for boxing in the depth of talent, the amount of activity, and the sport's unparalleled popularity. During that time, there were always strong punchers intent on knocking out opponents, but if that was their only dimension, they rarely ascended to contender status. There were far too many technically proficient boxers standing in their way who were satisfied to win on points. If the superior boxer saw an opportunity to score a knockout, he took it, but that was not the principal objective.

Every top contender of the 1920s to the 1950s would have been a dominant world champion today. The intense competition took place in only eight or ten weight divisions, and there were few split titles. At any one time, there were roughly two dozen contenders in each weight division who could beat the champion if he had an off night. This was especially true in the talent-filled lighter-weight divisions, from featherweight to middleweight.

Contenders and champions of the Golden Age knew how to capitalize on another fighter's mistakes because they could recognize the mistakes. The attitude of the elite boxers of the past was *I'm going to make this guy do what I want him to do. I'm going to make him fight my fight. I'm not going to fight his fight.* And they knew the moves to make that happen. As a result, the fights were more interesting to watch.

Today's champions have the heart, desire, and conditioning but haven't acquired the subtle skills of a true professional. I don't blame them. A lack of quality instruction impedes progress in any profession, and boxing is no different.

From ancient times to the present, one aspect of the sport has remained constant throughout its history—the boxer's vulnerability to brain trauma. That is why teaching and emphasizing the finer points of boxing technique is so important.

UNREALIZED POTENTIAL

There is much raw talent and unrealized potential among the thousands of professional boxers seeking fame and fortune. But under the present circumstances, even the best of them will never achieve the same type of training or depth of experience—and seasoning—acquired by the champions and contenders of the Golden Age. The arc of a professional boxer's career is much different today from what it was for boxers who came of age during the first half of the 20th century.[47] From the 1920s to the 1950s, boxers averaged sixty or more professional fights before winning a world title.[48] Today the average number of fights before winning a world title is twenty-one.[49]

Another major change that has affected the development of today's boxers is the way promoters, managers, and television have magnified the cost of defeat. Unlike their modern-day counterparts, Golden Age boxers were tested early in their careers against a variety of tough preliminary fighters before they graduated to main bout status. An occasional loss was considered an acceptable part of learning, provided the fighter was not too damaged in the process.

Today, maintaining an undefeated record is paramount. A loss must be avoided at all costs. To achieve this result, today's rising stars are carefully navigated and consistently matched against inferior opponents to make sure they have an undefeated record as they await a title shot. Consequently, they can't work through their flaws and show little improvement from their amateur days.

My friend Bill Goodman saw his first professional bout in 1947 and was a licensed cornerman with the New York State Athletic Commission from 1957 to 1966. He witnessed firsthand the changes that have harmed the sport over the past half century:

"Going back to the early 1900s, maybe earlier, the only thing that ever meant anything in boxing was a thorough effort on the part of the fighter. . . . Those two words 'thorough effort' are emphasized because of what they meant at the time. It was not whether you won or lost or fought to a draw. What was important was that you gave your best, and you gave your all, because if you did that, [promoters] would want to use you again. You developed a following because you put on a good show all the time. . . . You were better off losing a fight, and losing it properly, than winning the fight and stinking the joint out."[50]

With so many rising stars fearful of losing, the proper matches cannot be made because nobody wants to take a chance. The sport has never seen so many undefeated boxers with such high knockout percentages. The impressive records are taken at face value by many fans in the twenty-to-forty age range who don't realize the undefeated records are mostly a result of cherry-picking opponents.

Fans old enough to remember the moon landing are thankful they got to witness the genuine greats of that era: Ali, Frazier, Bob Foster, Roberto Duran, Carlos Monzon, Sugar Ray Leonard, Jose Napoles, Alexis Arguello, Marvin Hagler, Tommy Hearns, and Larry Holmes. In the 1990s and into the early 2000s, boxing still produced the occasional throwback fighter: Oscar De La Hoya, Pernell Whitaker, Lennox Lewis, Evander Holyfield, James Toney, Mike McCallum, Manny Pacquiao, and Floyd Mayweather Jr. were all extraordinary talents who would have stood out in any era. Who are the standouts today? Are any of them capable of offering us the same fleeting glimpse of a lost art?

LOMACHENKO, GOLOVKIN, AND CRAWFORD

Among the overcrowded field of mostly obscure champions recognized by the four major sanctioning organizations today are a few individuals who aren't cookie-cutter. These fighters stand out from the pack and are pleasing to watch because they show a higher level of skill than their contemporaries. Each has his own unique style of fighting that is reminiscent of their Golden Age predecessors. If Vasyl Lomachenko, Gennady Golovkin, and Terence Crawford had turned pro fifty years ago, it's possible they could have achieved true greatness, but we will never know.

Vasyl Lomachenko took ballet lessons as a youth and has footwork that's reminiscent of the great Willie Pep's. After a spectacular amateur career that included winning consecutive gold medals at the 2008 and 2012 Olympics, Lomachenko turned pro in 2013 and won his first world title (featherweight) in his third pro fight. Over the next four years, he won titles in both the super featherweight and lightweight divisions. But in ten years as a pro, Lomachenko has had only twenty fights. After ten years as a pro, Willie Pep had had 153. As in any profession, there is no substitute for experience.

Gennady Golovkin was a former middleweight and super-middleweight champion (2010–2022) at the end of a very successful career. In his prime Golovkin used a powerful left jab to set up damaging combination punches. He also understood the value of effective body punching. Undeniably crowd-pleasing, Golovkin's style combined awesome power with superior technique on both offense and defense.

Terence Crawford, who currently holds three of the four welterweight title belts (WBC, WBA, WBO), has great natural ability. But although he possesses speed, power, solid fundamentals, and great instincts, he can't be called a seasoned veteran. In fourteen years as a pro, he's had only thirty-eight fights (an average of 2.7 fights per year). Crawford recently moved up in weight to capture the WBO Interim World Super Welterweight title (154 pounds). But at age thirty-five, without having reached his full potential, Crawford is past his prime as a boxer.

If we could time-travel Golovkin, Lomachenko, and Crawford back several generations, they would be considered promising prospects but wouldn't yet be ready to challenge for a world title. While their unmistakable talent and potential would be recognized, so would their need for additional experience and testing against stiffer competition. The road to become a top contender or world champion would be much more challenging than the one they have traveled because in every decade from the 1920s to the 1950s there were *dozens* of Golovkins, Lomachenkos, and Crawfords vying for a chance at the title. The competition was brutal. To win a championship or achieve top-contender status when there were only eight weight divisions—and generally one undisputed champion for each—was an extraordinary achievement.

A STRIKING DIFFERENCE

Every year there are some two hundred Alphabet title belts up for grabs. It is not unusual for a single fight card to include several championship bouts. Before pro boxing became hopelessly fragmented, in the 1980s, and weight divisions and championships multiplied, it was extremely rare for a fight card to include more than one world title fight. Indeed, from 1920 to 1980, there were only six such cards, with the first taking place in 1937.[51]

In these days of degraded championships, just one year, 2022, saw six cards with multiple title fights.[52] One of those events took place at the Seminole Hard Rock Hotel and Casino, in Hollywood, Florida. Showtime broadcast the three championship fights. Each boxer's won-lost-draw record and how he fared in the title fight are shown next to his name.

August 21, 2022
- **Alberto Puello (20-0) won a 12-round decision, defeating Botirzhon Akhmedov (9-1). Title: WBA World Super Lightweight (135-pound limit).**
- **Sergey Lipinets (16-2-1) won a TKO-8, defeating Omar Figueroa, Jr. (28-2-1). Title: WBC Silver Super Lightweight (140-pound limit).**
- **Hector Luis Garcia (15-0) won a 12-round decision, defeating Roger Gutierrez (26-3-1). Title: WBA World Super Featherweight (130-pound limit).**

The first boxing card that included three undisputed title bouts took place in 1937 and was the brainchild of promoter Mike Jacobs. The fights were staged at the Madison Square Garden Bowl in Long Island City, New York.

September 23, 1937
- **Lou Ambers (68-5-6) won a 15-round decision, defeating Pedro Montanez (67-4-3). Title: Undisputed World Lightweight (135-pound limit).**

- Barney Ross (71-3-3) won a 15-round decision, defeating Ceferino Garcia (94-23-12). Title: Undisputed World Welterweight (147-pound limit).
- Harry Jeffra (45-3-1) won a 15-round decision, defeating Sixto Escobar (35-13-2). Title: Undisputed World Bantamweight (118-pound limit).

Compare the records of the fighters from the two cards. The difference is striking. In the three title bouts in 2022, the total number of fights for the six boxers ranges from ten to thirty-one, for a total of 125 bouts. Compare that to the 1937 card. The total number of fights for the six boxers there ranged from forty-nine to 129, for a combined total of 458. In addition, of the 125 opponents faced by the 2022 group, only thirty-six had had more than thirty professional fights. In the 1937 group, of their previous 458 opponents 378 had had more than thirty professional fights. But it is not just the number of fights that separates the eras; it is the quality of the competition. Among those 378 opponents were scores of battle-tested contenders and future hall of famers.[53]

WORDS OF WISDOM

Freddie Roach is not only one of boxing's best trainers; he also knows boxing history. "I think the art of boxing has changed over the years," he said. "I had fifty-four pro fights, the last one in 1987. Now, fifty-four fights is not a lot of fights compared to the guys back then. Years ago, guys fought two or three hundred pro fights in their career, and they really learned their craft. Experience is a great asset. We get better with age; we learn. . . . I don't think that fighters of today get that [opportunity] to learn."[54]

While emphasizing the virtues of experience, Freddie Roach regrets that he ignored his trainer, Eddie Futch, who told him to retire because he was past his prime and facing additional damage. Instead, he fought for three more years and is now afflicted with symptoms of chronic traumatic encephalopathy (CTE).

Former middleweight contender Wilbert "Skeeter" McClure expanded on this point when I interviewed him in 2006 for my book *The Arc of Boxing*. Before he turned pro, in 1960, McClure won every major amateur tournament, including a gold medal in the 1959 Pan American Games and a gold medal in the 1960 Rome Olympics. As a professional, McClure fought in the middleweight division from 1961 to 1967, taking on the likes of

Jose Torres, Luis Rodriguez, and Rubin "Hurricane" Carter. He retired with a 24-8-1 record to pursue a Ph.D. in psychology and went on to establish a successful practice. He also served as chairman of the Massachusetts Boxing Commission.

"Boxing, in my opinion, is the only sport in which the participants haven't gotten any better since the 1930s, '40s and '50s," said McClure. "Football players today are better than the ones who were playing in the '50s. It's the same with basketball and baseball. The fighters today couldn't even hold a candle to the fighters of the 1960s and '70s. . . . [The fighters of that era] were too tough, and too strong and too savvy and too skilled. Part of the reason is that they fought more frequently. You have champions today who fight once or twice a year. Anybody who applies his craft to any trade or profession and performs it only twice a year can't be good. You just cannot develop that way."[55]

Some might assume that because they fight less frequently, today's professional boxers are suffering less physical damage than the old-timers. I'm not so sure. By focusing on offense and not learning how to roll, ride, duck, or parry punches, or even how to clinch properly, today's boxers are walking into head shots and getting hit with more punches per round than their Golden-Age counterparts. And if they aren't being taught those moves in training, it means they're also getting hit too much in sparring sessions in the gym.

Even if today's fighters throw fewer punches per round than the old timers, which is arguable, they get hit more because they typically lack sophisticated defensive skills. If the CompuBox system of counting punches existed from the 1920s to the 1970s, it would have shown far fewer "power punches" connecting to the heads of the Golden Age's best fighters than the number of such punches rattling the brains of today's champions and contenders.

The old-timers would often fight once or twice a month. Their busy schedules required them to master defense; otherwise, they would have been too damaged to fight so often. Acquiring knowledge and experience were key to survival. The skills they acquired along the way allowed them to fight despite bruised hands or cuts and abrasions that hadn't fully healed.

Golden Age fighters didn't show CTE symptoms in their thirties or forties unless they had stayed around too long or had taken excessive punishment. In most cases, the more obvious symptoms didn't appear until they reached their sixties and seventies. In recent years, we have seen too many fighters in their thirties and forties already showing CTE symptoms, such as slurred speech and memory loss.

REVIVING THE JAB

A glaring indication of the lack of quality instruction is the virtual disappearance of the jab as an effective tool for offense and defense. When used properly, a left jab—or for a southpaw, a right jab—is boxing's most important and strategic weapon. And it's not just a point-scoring blow, but it also helps keep the opponent off-balance and creates openings for other blows. It can also be used as a feint.

A fighter with an effective jab has a great advantage. According to CompuBox statistics, in his last welterweight title fight, Terence Crawford landed 87 percent of 206 jabs, while Errol Spence landed only 11 percent of 296 jabs. Crawford stopped Spence in the ninth round. Although Crawford threw fewer jabs, he was more accurate, and his timing was superior.

Trainers owe it to their fighters to possess a thorough knowledge of boxing technique. At the very minimum, they should be required by their state or country's boxing commission to read approved instruction books and pass a test that reveals the extent of their knowledge and understanding of boxing technique and training. Reading a basic training guide that covers the fundamentals of boxing is better than not reading any, as long as the guide was written by someone with the right credentials. In a counterexample, *Weight Training for Boxers,* a book published about twenty years ago by a former power lifter, contains exercises using heavy weights that would make it hard to develop the speed and "snap" necessary for the sport and should be avoided. I find it telling, but not surprising, that, compared to recent times, many more worthwhile instruction books were published from the early 1900s to the mid-twentieth century, when boxing was part of the mainstream popular culture.

The incomplete content of contemporary boxing instruction books reflects the knowledge that has been lost. Some can be read as acceptable basic instruction manuals and do no harm, while others appear to be written by dilettantes possessing an extraordinarily limited knowledge of boxing fundamentals. But even the best of them wouldn't suffice to educate trainers. For that, we have to look to earlier volumes.

I began collecting vintage and modern boxing instruction books in the 1970s. Most were published in the early 1900s through the 1940s. Among

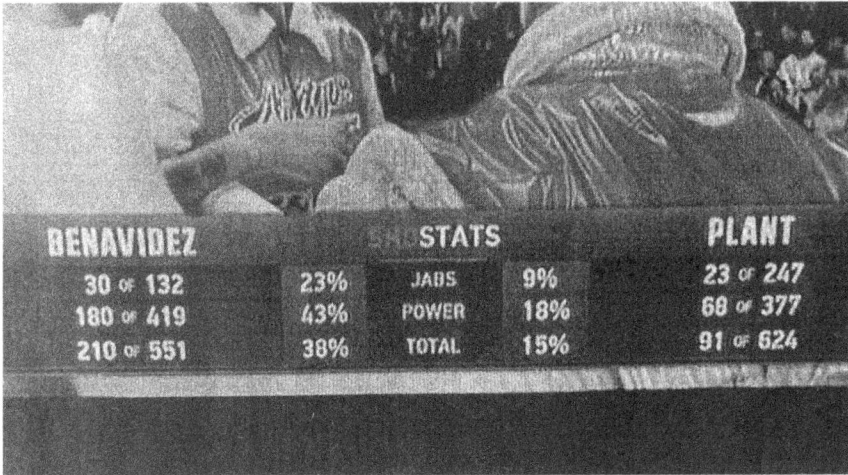

BENAVIDEZ		STATS		PLANT
30 of 132	23%	JABS	9%	23 of 247
180 of 419	43%	POWER	18%	68 of 377
210 of 551	38%	TOTAL	15%	91 of 624

Punch count statistics shown at the end of Plant–Benavidez reveal that today's boxers under-utilize the jab. Power punches often outnumber jabs by a factor of two or three. *Showtime*

the sixty instruction books in my collection is a reprint of *The Art of Manual Defense*, published in England in 1759, and believed to be the earliest published boxing instruction book. All of these books have something to offer, but the best of them appeared about eighty years ago.

In my opinion the best of all the instruction books is *Boxing: Naval Aviation Physical Training Manual*. It is one of a dozen naval aviation physical training manuals (others were written for wrestling, football, soccer, basketball, swimming, gymnastics, and military track) published by the United States Naval Institute. The boxing manual states that it was prepared "by the officers in charge of the instruction of Boxing in Naval Aviation," though it doesn't name them.

This remarkable 286-page illustrated compendium was developed in the early 1940s, around the outbreak of World War II with the purpose of building a standardized mass boxing program for naval aviation training. The idea was that acquiring boxing skills would confer large physical and psychological benefits, including, as explained in the preface of the revised edition, "qualities, such as quick reaction, coordination, accurate timing, tool judgment, aggressiveness, and determination."

What makes this book stand out is its abundance of detailed and correct information. For example, entire pages are devoted to expertly explaining and analyzing a single punch, with excellent accompanying photos. There are also sections on different types of feints and how to "draw a lead." These more sophisticated and rarely taught moves are appropriately placed toward the end of the book, as the boxer must first understand and master the basics, which are explained in earlier chapters. Each chapter ends with "coaching hints" that offer additional pointers. Reading the book is like having your own private old-school boxing coach. The book's authors had obviously been active in boxing in the 1930s and perhaps the 1920s. I doubt that such a book could be written today, given that so much knowledge pertaining to the finer points of technique has been forgotten.

Let's consider just one punch as described in the book—a left jab to the body (or for a southpaw a right jab to the body). That particular punch is rarely seen today, yet it used to be included in every good boxer's repertoire. No recent boxing instruction books—those published within the past thirty years—offer a detailed explanation of the mechanics of this punch. For example, a 118-page boxing instruction guide published in 2024 devotes just two and a half pages to the jab—including this perfunctory sentence: "[The jab is] the most common punch in boxing, with numerous variations, including the double jab, the triple jab, and the jab to the body." No further explanation follows. In the Navy book, by contrast, no fewer than five pages, including photos, are devoted to describing a jab to the body. Explained are the reasons to use it, the correct body alignment, feet and hand positioning, and how to defend against it. Here is a partial description excerpted from the book:

> Drop the trunk straight forward from the waist to a position approximately at right angles to the legs. The left leg bends slightly, the right leg more so. As the body drops, drive the left arm into forceful extension to the opponent's solar plexus. The blow is slightly upward, never downward. The right hand is carried high in front of the body ready for the opponent's left hook. Head should be held close to the extended left arm. Only the top of the head should be vulnerable to attack. *Never hold the position* but return as quickly as possible to the on-guard position.[56]

Below you'll find a photo of Sugar Ray Robinson (often called the greatest boxer who ever lived) perfectly executing this punch during his welterweight title bout with top contender Tommy Bell in 1946 at Madison

Square Garden. Robinson's position and balance are exactly as called for in the book. (The photo adorned the cover of my first book, *The Arc of Boxing*.)

Also impressive, and the book to read before tackling the highly detailed Navy manual, is the 120-page *Boxing* by Edwin Haislet. Originally published in 1940 as *Boxing: A Self-Instruction Manual*, it went out of print but was reissued in 1982 and again in 2016. Amazon no longer carries it, but reprints can be found on other sites. It functions as an excellent condensed version of the more detailed Navy book.

Sugar Ray Robinson jabs the body of top contender Tommy Bell in a 1946 title fight. Robinson's position, balance, timing, and accuracy were flawless. *Author's collection*

If every boxing trainer studied one or both books it would help immeasurably in creating a safer environment for fighters.

About one year ago, I was contacted by the well-known trainer of a world champion. I had never met him but knew his fine reputation in the sport. In an email, he explained that he'd just finished reading my book *The Arc of Boxing: The Rise and Decline of the Sweet Science* (published in 2008) and found it very informative.

He wanted to know if I could recommend an outstanding boxing instruction book that goes into greater depth than what was around. I didn't hesitate to recommend both books.

CHAPTER 9

Is There a (Ringside) Doctor in the House?

Boxing physicians should be selected from the elite of sports medicine physicians. All must have specialized training and experience in the recognition of head injuries, especially mild concussions. They must fully understand when it is prudent to stop a contest because of head blows.
—Robert Cantu, M.D.

When I was a teenager and still aspired to be a boxer, I watched a former highly rated heavyweight contender shadow box in the ring at Stillman's Gym in New York. Nothing in his movements looked unusual, but my old-school trainer turned to me and said, "He's a shot fighter." (A "shot fighter" is a boxer whose reflexes and coordination have deteriorated to the point where he could be hurt by a quality opponent.) "How can you tell?" I asked. "Look at his legs. You can tell if a fighter is shot by the way he's moving his legs," he responded. He was pointing out the slow and slightly stiff-legged gait of a shot fighter's legs, as opposed to the swift, sure, and energetic footwork of a prime athlete.

My trainer had been in boxing for over thirty-five years. He'd seen it all. Indeed, the former heavyweight contender took a bad beating in his next fight before getting knocked out in the tenth round against an ordinary opponent. He never fought again.

While most people wouldn't recognize a shot fighter, neither would most doctors, including most ringside doctors. At no time was this more evident than when—some twenty years later—doctors at the world-renowned Mayo Clinic determined that thirty-eight-year-old Muhammad Ali was fit to challenge Larry Holmes in an effort to regain his title. The Nevada State Athletic Commission had ordered the examination (the fight with Holmes was to take place in Las Vegas) because of the commission's concerns about Ali's health and what looked like signs of brain damage.

In their final report the Mayo Clinic doctors did cite evidence of neurological deterioration, including slurred speech, but nevertheless asserted that there were no specific findings that would prohibit Ali from fighting.[57]

The Mayo Clinic's decision had veteran boxing trainers shaking their heads in disbelief. The battery of medical specialists who examined Ali had failed to understand the difference between a person in good physical condition and a person in good *fighting* condition. While Ali's heart, lungs, blood pressure, and other vital signs indicated a middle-aged man in good health, he was, in the parlance of the trade, a "shot fighter," and for his own safety should not have been granted a license to fight.

To make matters worse, Ali's personal physician, in what was later deemed a misdiagnosis, told him before the fight that his slurred speech and lethargy came from a thyroid problem and prescribed pills for the condition. Ali, thinking that taking more thyroid pills than the prescription called for would give him more energy, doubled the dose on his own, which left him dangerously dehydrated on the eve of the fight.

Holmes dominated every round of the contest, while Ali was a shadow of the great fighter he had been in his prime. Landing punches at will to Ali's head and body, Holmes won the first eight rounds . In the ninth round, Ali threw just four weak jabs and spent most of the round leaning on the ropes as Holmes landed punch after punch. During that round a dejected Howard Cosell, doing ringside commentary for ABC-TV, exclaimed, "This fight must be stopped!"

Anyone watching the travesty, including Nevada boxing officials, knew the fight should have already been stopped, but no one wanted to take responsibility for ending the great fighter's career while he still could stand.

I have no doubt the referee would have stopped the fight if any other boxer had taken the same punishment. As for the ringside physicians? They might as well have been invisible. At no time during the bout did a doctor visit Ali's corner to check his condition.

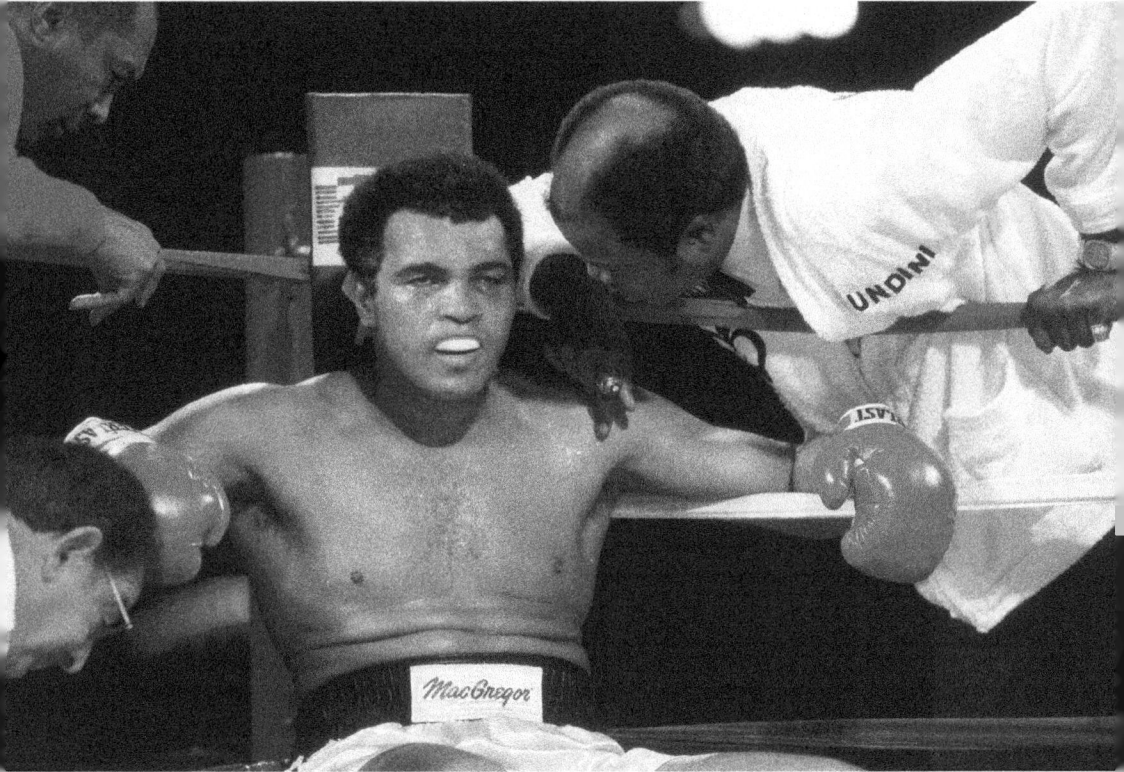

Exhausted, battered, and dehydrated, Muhammad Ali awaits yet another torturous round in his 1982 comeback fight against champion Larry Holmes. Even before the bout, the thirty-eight-year-old legend was experiencing symptoms of CTE. *Getty Images/Photographer: John Iacono*

Ali did not throw a single punch for the entire tenth round. Holmes, to his credit, began to ease up and pulled some of his punches as he realized that Ali had nothing left and was just a punching bag. The bell rang to end the round, and to everyone's great relief, Ali's corner finally told the referee to stop the fight.

Possessing a medical degree doesn't automatically prove that a doctor is qualified to work as a ringside physician. No one knows that better than Dr. Margaret Goodman, who came into the sport with a strong background in neurology. Dr. Goodman was a ringside physician with the Nevada State Athletic Commission (NSAC) from 1994 to 2005 and also served as the Nevada Commission's Medical Advisory Chairwoman from 2001 to 2007.

Though Dr. Goodman brought impeccable medical credentials to the post, she had to learn on the job how to be an effective ringside physician. A lot of that education was informal, and it was left up to her to self-educate.

No ringside physician should have to self-educate. The need for formal training is self-evident, especially in a sport whose occupational hazard is brain trauma.

Dr. Goodman considers the job of *ringside physician* to be a specialty, and that most doctors, including neurologists, are not qualified for it.

"In some respects a neurologist isn't the right person," she said. "In some respects an emergency room physician might be the best person to have on site. Another problem is when the ringside physicians don't do a good job in helping the referee make a determination, nobody says anything. . . . Physicians that do a bad job should not be involved, and there are plenty of them and no one does anything to stop that."[58]

Dr. Goodman—echoing Dr. Derby from chapter four—emphasized that a loss of consciousness does not have to happen for a concussion to occur. "Someone can function with a concussion, but continue to take punishment that can lead to permanent brain damage."[59]

Interviewed by author Tris Dixon for his book *Damage: The Untold Story of Brain Trauma in Boxing*, Dr. Goodman acknowledged the pressure on ringside physicians and referees. "If a medical doctor stops a fight, where the promoter has connections with the commission, you're never going to work another fight again," the doctor says. "Same thing for the referees, same thing for the judges. . . . The politics involved in the sport are probably just as important as the actual head trauma the fighters are taking because people don't want to step on other people's toes. There are too many outside influences, and the overall health of the sport has not improved as much as it could from those factors as well, which most people don't take into account."[60]

During her tenure with the Nevada commission, Dr. Goodman saw fighters she had banned in her state taken by promoters to fight in a state with less stringent medical standards. "It's frustrating because [the fighters] really are meat to them," she said. Asked about the prospects that the situation might improve, she said, "I can't, in my lifetime, imagine that's possible . . . In the

United States and worldwide, no one wants to give up a piece of the pie, irrespective of what the repercussions are to the fighters."[61]

Dr. Goodman left the NSAC in 2007, after being overruled when she tried to prevent a fighter she considered seriously damaged from fighting in another state. The fighter had passed a physical exam in that state and was allowed to fight there. (Dr. Goodman's authority did not extend beyond Nevada.)

She says, "One of the reasons I left the commission was because I wasn't able to make that determination, to say even though the tests are normal, this guy is in trouble and should not be licensed [in any state]. It was just too frustrating."[62] Unlike the Mayo Clinic doctors who gave a pass to Muhammad Ali, Dr. Goodman knew what a shot fighter looks like.

Tris Dixon believes Dr. Goodman is, in a way, another casualty of the blood sport: "Fighter safety will always be paramount [to Dr. Goodman], but it is sad to think that is one of the reasons why she is on the outside looking in. It's sad that, until only recently, she has not even been able to watch a fight on TV because she gets too annoyed."

Dixon added: "Boxing has left her with a severe case of burnout. It can happen when someone cares too much and spends their time shouting when no one cares to listen."[63]

After she left the Nevada commission, Dr. Goodman, still wanting to make a difference, founded the Voluntary Anti-Doping Association (VADA), which is considered the premier drug-testing agency in boxing and other combat sports.

STEPPING UP

Boxing safety would be improved if ringside physicians were encouraged by their state commission to take a more active role during a fight. But if their training is inadequate, how will they know when to intervene? This lack of knowledge may partly explain why so many ringside physicians remain in their seat.

In theory, the referee and ringside physician's responsibilities overlap, and they should work together. But too often the doctor stays on the sidelines of a fight, reluctant to interfere, leaving the bulk of responsibility to the referee. Doctors inclined to leave the decision of when to stop a fight solely to the referee are evading their responsibility.

Ringside physicians can be fans of the sport, as many are, but while working a fight they have to leave the fan's mindset behind. They must be always laser-focused on the action—and that includes watching each boxer as he returns to his corner at the end of a round, as well as keeping an eye on him during the one-minute rest period. I've often seen a fighter totter back to his corner on unsteady legs at the end of a round in which he has absorbed heavy punishment, yet the ringside physician stays in his seat. Or if the doctor decides to get a better look at a wobbly fighter, he'll stand on the ring apron, outside the ropes, craning his neck to peer over the cornermen's backs as they purposely move to block his view while they minister to the fighter's needs.

To avoid wasting valuable time, a better rule would be to give a competent doctor the authority to stop a contest *at any time* without having to go through the referee. Just a few extra punches—or even one punch—can cause irreparable damage to a fighter who can't any longer defend himself.

An even better solution would give the doctor seated at the ring apron access to a timekeeper's bell. Using the bell would alert the referee to immediately halt the action. In lieu of a bell, a loud air horn could be used—whatever quickly gets the referee's attention. If two qualified—the key word is *qualified*—ringside physicians are seated at opposite sides of the ring, both should have the authority to stop the fight if they see fit.

The referee bears a huge responsibility. The lives of the boxers are in his hands. Why should one person bear that responsibility alone? Understand: the referee is the key safety net. He can look into the fighters' eyes at any time and is close enough to them to see subtle changes that the doctor can't. The better the referee, the safer the fighters. Except in the case of a facial cut or severe nosebleed that may require the doctor's opinion, a competent referee shouldn't have to rely on a doctor to tell him when to stop a fight. But if the doctor decides the referee is letting the fight go on too long, it becomes the doctor's responsibility to quickly ask the referee to end it.

A downside to giving two doctors the freedom to end the bout is that some referees who fear being criticized as too cautious would prefer to let the doctors decide when to end the fight. That would be wrong and dangerous, no matter how qualified the ringside physicians. A referee should never use a doctor's authority to intervene as an excuse to avoid his own responsibility to act quickly where needed, based on his own judgment and experience.

The extra safety nets suggested in this chapter should be augmented by intensive, standardized training, testing, and certification for both ringside physicians and referees, primarily focused on how to recognize and deal with concussion during a professional boxing match. As of now, it is up to the individual ringside physicians, as well as individual referees, to seek out ways to increase their knowledge.

I recently learned of a certification program for ringside physicians involved in boxing and MMA. This online program is provided by the Association of Ringside Physicians (ARP), a voluntary, not-for-profit organization that has a current membership of about a hundred physicians worldwide. A certificate is awarded on completion of the online course. Annual membership for licensed physicians is $300 per year. State boxing commissions do not require their doctors to take the ARP's courses, although they can take them on a voluntary basis. Certainly, any online course that provides useful information is better than no training at all, but this course has not been independently evaluated and has not received the imprimatur of any boxing commission.

I have attended two of the ARP's annual conferences and was a guest speaker at the 2023 event. The conference took place at the Muhammad Ali Center in the former heavyweight champion's hometown of Louisville, Kentucky. I thought it both ironic and fitting that a conference of ringside physicians concerned about enhancing safety protocols should take place at a museum dedicated to a great fighter who can also be considered the poster person for brain damage in boxing.

Surprisingly, I came across a few doctors attending the ARP conference—mostly among those who'd been on the medical staff of a boxing commission for many years—who seemed uninterested in the topic of boxing safety. I don't even know why they were attending, unless it was just to take advantage of a few days' vacation. One doctor I met wanted absolutely nothing to do with boxing because of the frequency of brain damage among boxers. She was interested only in being a doctor for MMA contests. But thankfully other attendees seemed genuinely interested in seeking better ways to make boxing less dangerous, and felt responsible for protecting fighters' health. Boxing could undoubtedly use more of them.

CHAPTER 10

Too Much Flash and Too Little Substance

U
nlike the Association of Ringside Physicians, the thirty-plus-year-old Association of Boxing Commissions (ABC) has done nothing of significance to help solve professional boxing's myriad problems, including safety issues.

The not-for-profit organization has recently added the words "and Combative Sports" to its title to reflect the organization's interest in MMA and the emerging bare-knuckle scene, as well as gloved boxing.

The ABC's website claims the group "provides a framework for undertaking boxing and MMA bouts and record-keeping." *Framework* (as it applies to boxing) probably refers to their online "Boxing Referee Manual." At sixteen pages, it mostly lists rules and regulations, with only one page devoted to the topic of concussions. Other than an admonition for the referee to "observe the fighter's body language," it provides only a brief medical description of the signs of concussion. The rest of the manual covers, in far greater detail, the different types of fouls, scoring criteria, and such esoteric topics as proper dress codes for referees, judges, and fighters.

Meanwhile, the ABC's published *Unified Boxing Rules* is a near duplicate of the New York State Athletic Commission's rule book. And despite what their website claims, the ABC plays no part in record-keeping. The established go-to source for the records of boxers, past and present, is the BoxRec.com website. The ABC also claims to "promote uniform health and safety standards in boxing and MMA," but their actual impact and involvement in this area, as it relates to boxing, is insignificant.

If you detect dissatisfaction in my account of this organization, you aren't mistaken. What I find so frustrating is that, although they have about thirty-six state and tribal athletic commissioners as members, the ABC has never tried to organize them into an alternative to the pernicious sanctioning organizations that have caused so much damage to the sport and its athletes.

If the Association of Boxing Commissions really wanted to help the sport, it could take as its example the old National Boxing Association, a loose confederation of forty-three US boxing commissions that issued reliable ratings and sanctioned title fights from 1921 to 1962. If the ABC announced that they were taking over the role of the sanctioning organizations and would rate boxers and recognize as champion only those with the strongest claim to a title—while eliminating sanctioning fees—the WBC, WBA, IBF, and WBO would cease to be relevant. And if that were to happen, boxing fans worldwide would rejoice. The chance of that happening, however, is very small. The directors of the ABC have shown no interest in stepping into that role.

In the early 2000s, while doing research for my first book, *The Arc of Boxing*, I contacted the then-president of the ABC and asked why his organization didn't become more involved in cleaning up professional boxing. His answer? "We don't want to get involved with the politics of professional boxing." This person had a good reputation in the sport and had been active in his state's boxing commission for many years. I understood that his words had to do with the futility of trying to improve the infrastructure of a sport that has shown little interest in helping itself.

The ABC holds annual conferences at resort hotels in the United States. The conference I attended in 2022 took place at a very nice casino-hotel in Niagara Falls, New York. About two hundred commission staffers from throughout the United States showed up, many from states with few boxing shows but heavy MMA activity.

During the three-day conference, about twenty-seven lectures and classes were offered on various topics related to either boxing or MMA. Sessions included such topics as training for judges and inspectors (for both MMA and boxing), rules updates, suspension policies, transgender athletes in combat sports, fund-raising, new business, and combat sports law. Five of the classes involved safety issues: "Rapid Weight Loss," "Mechanics of the Knockout," "Concussion Testing," "Older Fighter Issues," "Boxing Deaths," and a two-hour referee course that included a test at the end.

Some of the safety courses offered good information, but they were sparsely attended. The two-hour boxing referee course, which I attended, was taught by a referee with a national reputation. It focused mostly on rules and responsibilities of the referee and less on how to recognize the signs and symptoms of concussion. Even so, it was worthwhile listening to this experienced referee, whom I consider a cut above the rest. However, I thought his talk could have been improved if it included video showing when a fight should be stopped. That type of filmed evidence, readily available, would say more than a thousand words. I was also disappointed to see that only fourteen people showed up for this lecture. Many more people attended the conference's social events, including a cocktail party and awards ceremony.

My overall impression is that the ABC, like much of boxing today, is mostly flash with little substance. Other than their unoriginal *Universal Rules* being the "go to" rule book for most boxing commissions, as they constantly boast, they've had a negligible impact on the sport of boxing. Of course, the directors of the ABC would disagree with this assessment. But one only has to look at their website to see that virtually all of their suggested rule changes in recent years involve MMA or bare-knuckle boxing. Even rule changes they've suggested for boxing in the past involved mostly insignificant tweaks to rules already enforced by most boxing commissions.

Looking at the ABC's history of past conferences there has never been any original significant rule changes suggested for professional boxing. However, in recent years there have been a flurry of rule changes pertaining to MMA and now bare-knuckle contests.

On the first day of the 2022 conference, I approached the current president of the ABC and asked why his organization never criticizes boxing's sanctioning bodies considering the many potentially dangerous mismatches the Alphabets approve. His reply was, "We have to work with these people." I wanted to clarify his answer—since their website claims the ABC "promotes safety standards in boxing and MMA"—but before I could continue the discussion the president quickly excused himself to attend to other matters.

Apparently, the ABC's directors are fanboys of the sport who've found a way to become a part of "the boxing club." They desire acceptance and recognition in that world, but ruffling the feathers of professional boxing's dominant players (major promoters and sanctioning organizations) is not part of their agenda, although I had difficulty figuring out exactly what their agenda was. Of course it's never easy to go against the tide, and much easier to accept the status quo if you want to be a member of the club.

After the conference, a statement appeared on the ABC's website, proudly announcing that the ABC was amending its "universal rules" by adding a new rule giving MMA fighters a five-minute timeout when on the receiving end of an accidental eye poke. (Most states allow the referee to decide how long a timeout the fighter needs after an accidental eye poke.) Another new rule gave MMA fighters permission to wear soft supportive neoprene sleeves to cover knee or ankle joints. It would still be up to the individual commissions that supervise MMA contests to implement these new rules. No mention was made of any rule changes for boxing. The rule changes for MMA are of minor importance and are already in place in certain jurisdictions. The pronouncements bespeak an organization that is trying to stay relevant while at the same time avoiding controversy.

The high point of the 2022 conference for many attendees was the appearance of the celebrity guest of honor, Mauricio Sulaiman, the "president for life" of the World Boxing Council (WBC)—Don King's favorite sanctioning organization. The ABC president's effusive praise for Sulaiman and his organization made it clear that the Association of Boxing Commissions and Combative Sports is not part of the solution for the ills of boxing. They are not even part of the problem for the simple reason that—as far as professional boxing is concerned—they are irrelevant.

CHAPTER 11

A New Scoring Protocol

*Two men parrying each other's blows and trying to box,
think, and will their way to victory make for an exhilarating
contest. One man beating on a defenseless opponent round
after round makes it brutal and boring.*
—Budd Schulberg

A few adjustments to professional boxing's scoring system can function as another safety net for fighters by providing an early-warning system to prevent unnecessary damage, including death. If one of the fighters is being dominated and out-punched consistently in every round, as reflected in the judges' scorecards, it should be seen as a danger signal by the referee and ringside physician, who would have to consider stopping the fight.

Even if a dominant fighter can't knock his opponent down, he can still cause significant brain trauma. In such a scenario, the three judges scoring the fight can play an important supporting role, as judges do in the following two situations:

❖ In amateur freestyle wrestling, if one of the wrestlers falls behind by fifteen points in the scoring, the referee will end the match owing to a lack of competitiveness. The rule has helped many overwhelmed wrestlers from being unnecessarily injured.

❖ Since 1992, when an Olympic boxer falls twenty points behind his opponent on the scorecards [according to a head punch count] the judges have the authority to advise the referee to stop the bout and save the outclassed boxer further punishment. (In pro boxing computerized head punch counts are not used for scoring, the judging is totally subjective.)

Professional boxing uses a "ten-point scoring system." Except in a round where a knockdown has occurred, most boxing judges automatically award ten points to who they determine to be the winner of a round and rarely fewer than nine points to the loser, even if one fighter has completely dominated the round and landed many more punches. Such a round would more accurately be scored 10-8 or 10-7. Nine points should be awarded to the loser of a round only when the round is actually close. Judges should also be more open to scoring a round even (10-10) if neither fighter has clearly won it. Most boxing judges seem incapable of understanding the difference between a 10-9 round and a 10-8 or 10-7 round, which is why they must be reeducated about proper scoring.

The fatal encounter between Maxim Dadashev and Subriel Matias in 2019 (described in chapter two) shows how a new rule, if properly implemented, might have saved a fighter's life.

Although too late to save Dadashev, his trainer, Buddy McGirt, stopped the fight after the eleventh round, at a time when the referee and ringside physician were ready to allow the bout to continue. The judges' scorecards weren't disclosed to the public, but the unofficial ringside scorer gave Dadashev only three of the previous eleven rounds. Although he stayed on his feet in them, rounds seven, nine, and ten were especially one-sided and punishing to Dadashev. The eleventh round was even worse, as he took one hard punch after another. The ringside television commentator said Matias was "teeing off" on Dadashev and had landed fifty-three of 142 punches. I have no doubt the judges scored that round 10-9 for Matias, but even without a new scoring protocol, this fight should have been stopped much earlier. More realistic scoring by the judges and a new rule that would automatically end a bout if one of the fighters has lost three rounds by two or more points would have prevented Dadashev from going out for the eleventh round, and it probably would have saved his life despite the referee and doctor's incompetence.

Of course, the fight would have also ended earlier if it was scheduled for eight rounds, as it should have been, considering the experience and history of both fighters (see chapter three).

INCENTIVIZING SKILL

Most boxing commissions observe the rule that automatically scores a round 10-8 in favor of a fighter who knocks down his opponent, even if he would have lost the round had he not scored the knockdown. In other words, if a boxer has dominated a three-minute round for two minutes and fifty-eight seconds but suffers a flash knockdown just before the bell, he automatically loses the round. Under the new rules I'm proposing, his opponent would be awarded just one point for the knockdown. But the opponent could still lose the round if, absent the knockdown, it would otherwise have been scored 10-8. This proposed rule would promote a higher level of skill by deemphasizing the importance of a knockdown in the scoring.

CHAPTER 12

Amateur Boxing versus Professional Boxing and the Head Guard Debate

Rom the 1890s to 2011, there were 1,604 boxing-related fatalities.[64] Of that number 273, or 15 percent, involved amateur fighters.[65] The most recent statistics from 2018 to 2022 show eighteen professional and six amateur deaths (two amateurs died as a result of sparring in the gym).[66]

There are thousands more amateur boxers than professionals, yet proportionally there are fewer annual deaths in amateur boxing than in the pros. That is because properly certified amateur programs take greater caution to ensure boxer safety. In addition, amateur fights are limited to three rounds (each lasting two or three minutes), while professional fights are scheduled from four to twelve three-minute rounds.

According to the rules of amateur boxing, if a boxer is momentarily stunned by a single punch or a series of punches, the referee will immediately call a halt and give a standing eight count. (See chapter six for the pros and cons of the standing eight count.) Amateur referees will stop a fight more quickly than their counterparts in the pros if it appears that a mismatch is taking place. The limited number of rounds also make it less likely that amateur boxers will experience the symptoms of CTE so common to professional boxers.

Despite the effort to make amateur boxing as safe as possible, it is still a dangerous contact sport, but much less so than its professional counterpart. A person who is either physically or mentally unfit to compete as a professional boxer is weeded out very early in the amateurs. When an amateur boxer is fatally injured, either in sparring or in an actual contest, the cause is most often an existing but undiagnosed medical condition, such as a brain aneurysm. When a professional boxer is fatally injured, it is rarely due to an underlying congenital disorder.

When two professional boxers in top physical condition are evenly matched for the right number of rounds and compete under the supervision of a qualified referee, the chance that one will be fatally injured is small. If there is a fatality, it is most often caused by severe punishment compounded by abuse, incompetence, or negligence on the part of the referee and other officials.

Another significant difference between amateur and professional boxing involves the use of a head guard, a foam-filled leather helmet that fits over the head. Most cover the forehead, temples, and ears but leave the jaw exposed. (Design variations include covering for the cheeks and jaw.) Their main purpose is to reduce the impact of a punch and prevent facial cuts and contusions. Invented in the late 19th century, head guards are used by amateurs and professionals when they spar in the gym. Most amateurs, and no professionals, are required to wear head guards during competition.

From 1906 to 1980, amateur boxers who competed in the Olympic Games were not required to wear head guards. In 1983 however, the International Boxing Association (IBA) introduced headgear in response to public outcry over the violence of boxing following the death of Duk Koo Kim. The South Korean boxer succumbed to injuries suffered in a title bout broadcast live on network television.

Thirty years later, in 2013, the International Olympic Committee reversed itself and ruled that head guards would *not* be mandatory for male boxers competing in the 2016 Olympic Games. Since then, other amateur boxing federations have made head guards optional for competition. The surprise decision by the IOC was based on research conducted by an IBA medical official, who himself warned that his findings were "preliminary." According to his study, referees had stopped matches for head injuries more often when boxers *were* wearing headgear, which seems counterintuitive.[67]

Not surprisingly, the absence of head guards for Olympic competition in the 2016 games resulted in a sharp increase in the number of facial injuries that would otherwise have been preventable had head guards been mandatory. Nevertheless, many amateur boxing federations have since made head guards optional for competition.

Most amateur boxers are required to wear a head guard while competing.
Radharc Images/Alamy Stock Photo

The Olympic Committee's decision to ban head guards at the world's premier amateur boxing tournament ignited controversy. Dr. Robert Cantu is one of the world's foremost authorities on brain trauma in sports and a clinical professor of neurology and neurosurgery. He is also the cofounder of the CTE Center at Boston University School of Medicine. Dr. Cantu said the IBA study was too small to reach an accurate conclusion, and that a larger study undertaken by doctors unaffiliated with the IBA was needed.[68] Agreeing with Dr. Cantu is Cynthia Bir, Ph.D., a University of Southern California biomechanics researcher who has evaluated boxing equipment for USA Boxing (the national governing body for Olympic-style boxing). "The only way to end conflicting opinion on whether wearing headgear reduces the incidence of concussions would be to conduct a comprehensive study," said Dr. Bir. "But whether ditching headgear actually makes boxing safer—especially from nonconcussive injuries—is, well, more complicated. There's still a lot of research that needs to be done."[69]

In 2015 an Australian biomechanical study concluded that current IBA-approved headgear can substantially reduce the risk of concussion and superficial injury in boxing competition and training.

The study found significant reduction in peak linear and angular accelerations during an impact and concluded that wearing headgear can "play an important role in reducing the risk of concussion." The study also showed there is a chance that those wearing a head guard could develop a concussion because at some point the force of a punch can overcome the protective capability of the head guard. In other words, wearing it will not prevent all concussions, but it can significantly decrease their likelihood.[70]

Another study, published in the *British Journal of Sports Medicine*, clearly showed that wearing headgear can decrease the force of a blow, but it did not decrease the incidence of concussion. The study also raised concerns that wearing headgear could reduce peripheral vision (easily corrected with a design adjustment), or create a false sense of safety, encouraging boxers to take more risks.[71]

Despite the mixed results of studies, Dr. Cantu believes there is reason enough for amateur boxers to continue wearing head guards: "Does it protect against concussion? Obviously not. Does it protect against getting CTE? Obviously not. Does it give you some protection attenuating blows to the head? Yes, so I think for the reason of protecting what you know it does—the face, the eyes, the cuts—that alone is reason to wear headgear. The marginal protection it gives you beyond that, for the brain, is probably the concept lesser is always better. So it's not protecting in any big way, but it's giving you some protection, and I would suggest it is worn."[72]

A recent analysis of thirty-nine articles dealing with headgear concluded that wearing a head guard does protect well against facial bruising and lacerations, while less is known about the protective effects against concussion and other traumatic brain injuries.[73]

No current studies conclusively demonstrate the protective effect of a head guard in relation to concussions. Nevertheless, after considering the available research, and weighing the pros and cons, I conclude, with Dr. Cantu, that wearing a head guard should be mandatory for fighters in all professional bouts. A concussion can be mild or severe. If wearing a head guard lessens the severity of a punch to the head, would it not help to reduce the severity of a concussion?

The NFL has invested millions of dollars to come up with a football helmet that offers better protection for their players. It's time for a similar gold-standard study to determine whether wearing a well-designed boxing helmet can significantly reduce the incidence of concussions. It could be easily funded by taking a small percentage of the profits from just one multimillion-dollar pay-per-view fight. But it's doubtful the boxing industry would agree to this. Promoters are not eager to contribute money to such a study because they fear reducing the brutality of boxing would alienate a large chunk of their audience. From their point of view, and that of many fans, even if the helmet allowed the chin to remain exposed, thereby making knockouts possible, wearing one would make the fighters look too much like amateurs.

An accidental or deliberate headbutt can cause more damage than a punch. Fritzie Zivic (right) headbutts Jake LaMotta (1943). *Author's collection*

The promoters' likely resistance aside, there are three compelling reasons for boxers to wear a head guard in professional fights, and no scientific tests are needed to support them. First, wearing a head guard will reduce the risk of brain injury from head collisions, which sometimes do more damage than the hardest punch.

An unintended severe clash of heads in the ninth round likely contributed to the near-fatal brain injury to Gerald McClellan in his ill-fated title bout with Nigel Benn in 1995. In the round that followed the collision of heads, McClellan began blinking furiously—a possible sign of brain injury. He purposely took a knee and allowed himself to be counted out. A few moments later, he became unconscious. McClellan had suffered a massive blood clot to the brain and underwent an emergency three-and-a-half-hour procedure to remove the clot. The surgery saved his life, but after two months in a coma he was left blind, hearing impaired, brain-damaged, and unable to walk. McClellan could have been protected from the devastating injury if

Gerald McClellan takes a knee in the tenth round, shortly after suffering a severe accidental headbutt in his brutal bout with Nigel Benn in 1995. *PA Images/ Alamy Stock Photo*

he'd worn a standard head guard, which exposes the chin but covers the head and temples with a foam cushion from the eyebrows up to the hairline.

A second reason to wear a properly designed head guard is to prevent a coup contrecoup concussion, which occurs when a boxer falls backwards after being hit and the back of his head slams against the ring floor, resulting in a secondary impact injury. While most head guards do not include a padded cushion that protects the back of the head, they could be modified to include this protection, with a two-inch layer of foam covering the back of every head guard.

Third, head guards prevent cuts and swelling that occur on or around the eyebrow ridge. Many bouts have been forced to end prematurely when a boxer suffers that type of injury. In one of the most notable examples, from 2003, Vitaly Klitschko, a 4-1 underdog, appeared to be on the verge of upsetting heavyweight champion Lennox Lewis, but was forced to retire at the end of the sixth round because of severe cuts above his left eye. Klitschko required sixty stitches to repair the damage.

The fact that additional research is needed to assess the protection that head guards can provide should not rule out their use for now. Head guards can reduce the impact of a headbutt, lessen the possibility of a secondary contrecoup injury (as described above), and prevent stoppages due to cuts —all of which make a strong case for their use in amateur *and* professional boxing.

Many fans of pro fighting oppose head guards because they're too reminiscent of amateur boxing. Perhaps a compromise can be reached that would address this concern and make it more acceptable to boxing fans.

Why not, for example, create a less obtrusive head guard with a streamlined design that would still allow for knockouts but significantly lessen or eliminate the damage caused by headbutts, coup countrecoup concussions, and stoppages due to cuts? This head guard would be unique to professional boxing and similar in size and shape to a sweat headband. It would consist of a circular foam-filled pad that would extend from the eyebrows to the hairline (about four inches). The boxer's face, including the chin, cheeks, and ears would be exposed. The head guard would be secured by a strap that buckles under the chin. The area of the pad covering the forehead would be one inch thick. The part that covers the back of the head would be two inches thick and extend six inches in length to offer protection from illegal and potentially lethal rabbit punches delivered to the base of the skull.

In fact, a head guard very similar to this already exists and is available for soccer players in the hope that it reduces the risk of concussions and other head injuries (see photo).

Though it is not widely worn, FIFA, the international self-regulatory governing body for soccer, first allowed the use of protective headgear (often called "concussion headgear") on the soccer field in 2003.[74] With slight modifications the headgear available to soccer players can be reengineered for pro boxing.

Although I favor head guards, I'm not saying they are a panacea. Boxers have been killed or suffered permanent brain damage while wearing a head

With minor adjustments this soccer helmet can be adapted for professional boxing. It would protect against head butts, cuts, and coup contrecoup concussions. *Storelli.com*

guard, but how many others could have been saved if wearing one was mandatory for all professional and amateur bouts? More studies are needed to determine whether head guards prevent or diminish concussions.

I realize that fans may dislike head guards, but I believe their adoption would be worthwhile if boxing commissions mandated that a percentage of all professional prizefights be fought with them for one year. After a year the commissions can evaluate the results and decide whether to make a head guard mandate permanent.

● ● ●

One hundred and thirty years ago, the Marquess of Queensberry rules took a page from amateur boxing and ordered all boxers to wear padded leather gloves. The new rule effectively ended the brutal bare-knuckle era. Many fans of bare-knuckle boxing were upset with the change, believing that fighting with gloves on was a poor substitute for "the real thing." But they were wrong. The essence of the sport remained, and it became more popular than ever. A new generation of fans emerged who knew only gloved boxing and saw it as completely normal.

If a soccer helmet modified for boxing—as described above—became mandatory, the next generation of boxing fans would readily accept it.

CHAPTER 13

The Boxing Brain versus the Football Brain

The human brain is not designed to be punched repeatedly.
The long-term consequences of such trauma can be devastating.
—Robert Cantu, M.D.

I n the 1920s neurologists established that CTE (chronic traumatic encephalopathy) was not uncommon in professional boxers. At the time the general public knew the condition by a different name: "punch drunk." People used this pejorative term to describe ex-boxers who exhibited slurred or garbled speech, awkward movement, Parkinson's tremors, memory loss, and other degenerative changes that in later years often was followed by full-blown dementia. More than seventy years later, Dr. Bennet Omalu, a forensic neuropathologist, discovered CTE in NFL players. The story of Dr. Omalu's CTE research and the pressure he faced from the NFL to disavow his work inspired the feature film *Concussion*.

Over the past two decades, an increasing number of NFL players have reported symptoms consistent with CTE. In a 2017 study published by the *Journal of the American Medical Association*, the condition was diagnosed in 110 of 111 former players whose brains had been donated for research. (A diagnosis of CTE can be confirmed only by a postmortem examination of the brain.) All the brains studied showed various stages of CTE.[75] Two years later, another study, led by Dr. Ann McKee, a leading authority in the field of head trauma, was published in the *Annals of Neurology* medical journal. The study reported CTE in the brains of 223 of 266 football players.[76]

Most recently, researchers at the Boston University CTE Center analyzed the brains of 376 deceased NFL players. They found that 345 of them—about 92 percent—had CTE.[77]

The brains of professional boxers don't fare much better than those of the NFL players. According to the Association of Neurological Surgeons, nearly 90 percent of boxers suffer a brain injury of some degree during their career.[78] Up to 40 percent eventually develop chronic impairment, or CTE.[79]

Despite some overlap in symptoms, including headaches, memory problems, and dementia, the slurred speech common to brain-damaged boxers is rarely seen in retired NFL football players, even those who've had long careers.

Researchers believe the difference may be due to the location of the lesions within the brain. While CTE damages the brains of both boxers and football players, some brain areas are more affected in boxers and others are more affected in football players. This likely has to do with the way each type of athlete becomes injured. When a boxer's bandage-wrapped-glove-encased fist slams into the jaw of an opponent, the result is a rapid rotational acceleration of the head either to the left or the right. The primary impact is to the side—the temporal area—of the brain, the part most responsible for speech.

In American football the athlete's entire body can be used as a weapon. Data compiled by researchers at Stanford showed that one college offensive lineman sustained sixty-two hits in a single game.[80] Contact came with an average force on the player's head equivalent to what you would see if he had driven his car into a brick wall at thirty miles per hour.[81]

Unlike the rotational impact of a punch, the violent collision of bodies involved in football tackling causes an asymmetric movement of the head forward, back, or to the side. And if a player gets hit by more than one opponent at the same time, extreme shearing forces on the brain can result. The part of a football player's brain most often affected is the frontal lobe rather than the temporal area. The frontal lobes are considered the emotional control center, involved with memory, judgment, impulse control, and social behavior.

In 2005 Mike Webster, an NFL center from 1974 to 1990, became the first National Football League player to be diagnosed with CTE. Some doctors speculated that Webster had been in the equivalent of "twenty-five thousand automobile crashes" in over twenty-five years of playing football at the high school, college, and pro levels. Webster died at age fifty from a heart attack. At the time he was living out of his pickup truck and suffering from amnesia, dementia, depression, and erratic behavior.[82]

• • •

A recent study showed that from 2009 to 2015 eleven current and former professional football players committed suicide. Although proportionally not higher than the frequency of suicide for men in their age group, football athletes are reported to have the highest suicide rate of athletes in all sports.[83]

Several of the suicides made national headlines. The posthumous brain examination of Phillip Adams—a thirty-two-year-old retired NFL player who shot and killed six people before dying by suicide in April 2021—showed significant dense lesions in both frontal lobes, an abnormally severe diagnosis for a person in his thirties.[84] It was the diagnosis that most nearly resembled that of Aaron Hernandez, a former New England Patriots tight end who was twenty-seven years old when he died by suicide, after being convicted in 2013 of murder and sentenced to life in prison. In 2012 Jovan Belcher, a twenty-five-year-old former All-American college player who played in the NFL for three years, killed his twenty-two-year-old girlfriend and then shot himself. A medical examiner's report determined that Belcher had suffered from CTE.[85] Of course, these are extreme examples, and while it is true that very few ex-NFL players with CTE have committed suicide or murder, many suffer from symptoms that include depression, erratic behavior, and thoughts of suicide.

The well-publicized revelations of CTE in football players and a multimillion-dollar class action lawsuit brought by the players against the NFL spurred the organization to make dozens of new rules that aim to eliminate dangerous tactics and reduce the risk of injuries. These include a rule that makes it illegal for a player to deliver a blow to the head with his helmet, forearm, or shoulder.

The league also created a list of "Game Day Protocols." Developed in 2011 by the NFL Head, Neck, and Spine Committee—a board of independent and NFL-affiliated physicians and scientists—the Game Day Protocols aim to lower the incidence of serious brain injury. Whenever a player shows any sign or symptom suggestive of a concussion, such as dizziness, balance or motor instability, amnesia, nausea, disorientation, vertigo, or cognitive slowness, he is immediately removed to the sidelines or stabilized on the field and assessed for concussion. The results of that assessment will determine whether he's removed from the game and escorted to the locker room for further observation.[86]

One protocol that is considered absolutely vital involves keeping the player out of the game to avoid "second impact syndrome," which occurs when a second concussion is sustained before complete recovery from a previous concussion. Another concussion so soon after the first one can lead to cerebral swelling and irreversible neurological damage.

Recently the concussion protocol was revised to account for ataxia, the medical term for the poor muscle control associated with concussions, which can appear as unsteadiness or slurred speech. Going forward, any player diagnosed with ataxia will not be allowed to return to the game.

The NFL also requires every player to have a baseline neurocognitive test to be used in evaluating the player if he is suspected to have sustained a concussion during the season, either in practice or an official game.

It is much easier for the National Football League to adjust its rules and conduct the type of medical testing and monitoring described above than it would be for professional boxing, a sport that lacks a national commissioner or any centralized authority. Further complicating the challenge is the fact that in boxing, unlike the other sports, the main target is the head, and hurting your opponent is a goal. After all, a knockout, the most desired result in boxing, is another word for concussion, and repeated blows to the head are as much a part of boxing as field goals are to basketball.

The safest way for a boxer to lose is by a knockout from one punch in the first few seconds of round one, which would avoid the repetitive brain jarring and irreversible damage caused by second-impact syndrome that can occur in a longer fight.

• • •

From a medical testing perspective, is the boxing industry doing enough to protect its athletes? According to Ted Lidsky, Ph.D., a former amateur boxer who is also a neuroscientist, the answer is no. Dr. Lidsky, who's been involved with brain research for over fifty years and has examined many retired boxers, believes the rate of boxers suffering from CTE is much higher than the 40 percent estimate put forth by the Association of Neurological Surgeons.

"In my opinion no one escapes, not a single one," he says. "There are fighters who seem to be OK later on—for example Jake LaMotta [the former middleweight champion from 1949 to 1951]. Some can appear to be lucid and functional, but as far as what they could have been I'm almost certain it's reduced. As they get older, memory will fade faster than it normally would in age-related memory loss. Their cognitive functions will be less, with more difficulty problem solving, more difficulty performing activities in daily living, more problems with planning, more so than they would have had if they'd not had their head concussed numerous times.

"There are some who can compensate very well, especially if they were particularly intelligent. But I don't think anybody gets away without brain injury. In my opinion everybody who has a full career in boxing suffers some persistent detriment that lasts their entire life. No one escapes."

What does he consider a full career?

Lidsky: "These days, the way fighters fight with their face, ten fights is enough. And it's not just ten fights. It's all the training that goes into it. Most have amateur careers and all the training that goes into it. Right from the beginning, they get hit with too many punches. Fans today are so fixated on punch counts. They ought to try doing punch counts from films of the fighters from the '40s and '50s and compare to current fighters at the championship level, and look at the difference in the number of punches that connect to the head."

Dr. Lidsky believes using better diagnostic tools could make a difference when monitoring the fighter's brain health.

"For example, they should be using functional scans, rather than MRIs or CAT scans, to try to detect brain injury. Because the kind of brain injury from head trauma doesn't show up on a CT scan or MRI until it's far too late. But it will show up on a so-called functional scan immediately."

I asked the doctor how a functional scan differs from an MRI.

"The difference is that in addition to showing the structure of the brain, it will also show whether the structure is actually functioning. For example, if you ask a person to do a certain task, certain parts of the brain of a normal person should become active and will show up on a functional MRI. So, if there is a question of an injury, or not, you can see if the brain is being activated normally.

"Another method to identify whether or not there has been a brain injury - a method that does not require a scan - is neuropsychological testing. This methodology consists of paper-and-pencil tests and computer exercises. It may well be more sensitive to brain injury than are scans."

Is there anything new, or in the experimental stages, that address the problem?

"There are drugs called neuroprotective agents that are being developed to counteract the effects of any kind of blunt force injury to the brain. They would try to minimize inflammation and other processes that go along once the brain has been injured. There is a big effort to develop such drugs, but they are still in the experimental stage and there have been no clinical trials so far."[87]

• • •

Although a knockout is the most obvious sign of a concussion, a boxer can still suffer brain damage without ever being knocked out or even knocked down. Muhammad Ali was stopped only once but never actually knocked out. CompuBox, a company that compiles punch count statistics examined the films of forty-seven of Ali's sixty-one professional bouts, and concluded that he was hit with over seven thousand punches. That number doesn't include Ali's more than one hundred amateur bouts or the countless times he was hit while sparring an estimated twelve thousand rounds as part of his training regimen.[88]

Ali survived the poundings but ended up with profound brain damage. He began to show obvious symptoms of CTE in his late thirties, which is early even by boxing standards. The condition took its natural course, worsening every year. By age sixty this once vibrant and loquacious personality was reduced to a shuffling, whispering, shaking wreck who could no longer care for himself.

Ali was forty-two years old when diagnosed with Parkinson's disease, in 1984. Research shows a strong correlation between repeated head trauma and an increased risk of Parkinson's. Experts believe that the repeated blows to the head Ali received during his career significantly increased his risk of developing Parkinson's disease. However, a definitive diagnosis of CTE, although highly likely, could not be arrived at, as Ali's family declined a post-mortem neuropathological examination of his brain

At the time of his last bout, Ali was thirty-nine years old and way past his prime. He had stayed far too long in his dangerous profession. Yet despite the terrible cumulative damage caused by all the punches he took, Ali never became violent or suicidal. The same can be said of Sugar Ray Robinson, Floyd Patterson, Jerry Quarry, Aaron Pryor, Leon Spinks, Bobby Chacon, Wilfredo Benitez, Meldrick Taylor, and many other former ring stars. They all suffered the debilitating effects of too many punches to the head. But no matter whether damage occurred in a boxing ring or on the gridiron, or how and when it manifested itself, the end result for the athlete diagnosed with CTE is progressive mental deterioration.

Sadly, professional boxing lags behind the NFL in shielding its participants from severe brain damage. Unless meaningful and worthwhile changes are made, boxing will continue to fall short of its responsibility when it comes to the well-being of its athletes.

CHAPTER 14

Boxing versus Mixed Martial Arts: Which Sport Is More Dangerous?

The experienced viewer understands that a boxer's
bleeding face is probably the least of his worries.
—Joyce Carol Oates

In 1993, a new sport emerged called Mixed Martial Arts (MMA), which has become very popular both in the United States and internationally. As noted in chapter three, MMA is exactly what its name implies: a full-contact hybrid sport that allows for a variety of fighting techniques from boxing, wrestling, judo, jiu-jitsu, kickboxing, and other combat sports. MMA rules allow both striking and grappling techniques that can be used while fighters are standing or on the ground. Competition is usually conducted in an octagonal, fenced enclosure, which is why the sport is also referred to as "cage fighting." The standard cage, known as the Octagon, has a diameter of thirty feet.

MMA fighters wear 4-ounce leather gloves that cover the knuckles and wrist but leave the fingers exposed for grappling. Most bouts are limited to three rounds of five minutes each with, as in boxing, a one-minute rest period between the rounds. Title fights and main events are limited to five five-minute rounds. MMA fighters can win by judges' decision, by knockout, or by submission. Submission requires the fighter to acknowledge defeat by tapping his opponent or the mat (known as "tapping out"), or by verbally notifying the referee. This usually occurs when a fighter is caught in a painful

Studies show that while MMA fighters face a slightly higher risk of minor injuries, boxers are more likely to experience serious and long-term harm from concussions. *Richard Arthur/Alamy Stock Photo*

hold he cannot break free from, or when he's being choked and about to pass out.

A knockout in MMA differs from a regulation boxing knockout in that there is no "ten count." In fact, there is no count at all. In a move that would get a boxer immediately disqualified, an MMA fighter who knocks down his opponent with a punch, kick, or throw is allowed to continue to pummel the downed fighter's head with his fists until the referee intervenes. (In MMA lingo, this is known as "ground and pound.") If a fighter loses consciousness—even for a second—from a punch, kick, or choke hold, or if he looks as if he can't defend himself, the referee will quickly interrupt the attack and end the match. The referee's swift action aims to avoid further injury.

If all this sounds quite violent, it is. But there are limits to the mayhem. An MMA fighter can lose by disqualification if he fouls an opponent, and fouls include hitting below the belt, kicking or knee-striking the head of a grounded opponent, headbutts, strikes to the back of the head or spine, eye gouging, pinching or twisting the flesh, and biting. Most bouts rarely end on a foul.

On the surface MMA contests can appear more brutal and dangerous than professional boxing, especially in the event of a ground-and-pound. But is it really? Recent studies have shown that, while MMA fighters suffer more broken bones, torn ligaments, and facial contusions, professional boxers suffer more brain trauma. In 2015, researchers at the University of Alberta's Glen Sather Sports Medicine Clinic discovered that while MMA fighters face a slightly higher risk of minor injuries, boxers are more likely to experience serious harm from concussions and other head trauma, including loss of consciousness and eye injuries. These are the injuries that matter most to one's long-term health.

The Alberta researchers studied post-fight medical data of 1,181 MMA fighters and 550 boxers who competed from 2003 to 2013 in Edmonton, Alberta. The study found that 59 percent of MMA fighters and 50 percent of boxers suffered some form of injury during their bout. However, 7 percent of boxers lost consciousness or suffered serious eye injuries, compared to 4 percent of MMA fighters. Additionally, boxers were "significantly more likely" to receive post-bout medical suspensions for their injuries, which also suggests a higher likelihood of serious injuries in boxing.[89]

A survey conducted in 2022 by the Professional Fighters Brain Health Study involving 131 MMA fighters, ninety-three boxers, and twenty-two controls found that when comparing brain volumes "significant differences were seen between boxers and MMA fighters, including lower brain volumes than the MMA fighters." Lower brain volume indicates a loss of neurons and supporting cells, which is most often seen in the brains of the elderly, and rarely in persons in their twenties or thirties. The study concluded:

Perhaps the most obvious explanation is that boxers get hit in the head more. In addition to trying to concuss (knock out) their opponent, MMA fighters can use other combat skills such as wrestling and jiu-jitsu to win their match by submission without causing a concussion. In a review of sixty consecutive fights within the 125 to 145-pound weight class, punch-count statistics for the fights showed that boxers received, on average, 175 total punches per fight compared to fifty-eight for MMA fighters.[90]

To anyone familiar with the mechanics of both MMA and professional boxing, the results of the studies are not surprising. Despite MMA's reputation as one of the most brutal and bloodiest of all contact sports, in reality boxing poses a greater risk of CTE. The MMA fighter's face may be bloodied and bruised, his nose may be broken, and he may lose more blood, but he faces less repetitive head punishment when compared to boxers.

Although some MMA fighters can punch with power, those who go into the sport with a wrestling or judo background have an advantage once the action goes to the mat. In a boxing match the competitors do not have to concern themselves with being kicked or thrown to the mat. They are totally focused on landing or defending against punches, most aimed at the head. MMA fighters attempt far fewer punches (and with less effect) than boxers do. And they tend to avoid punching or evading punches from certain angles because they don't want to get grabbed or kicked

Unlike MMA refs, who immediately stop the fight if an MMA fighter loses consciousness from a punch or kick to the head, or through a choke hold, boxing referees count to ten seconds over the fallen fighter. (As per the rules the opponent goes to a neutral corner while the count proceeds.) Even if a downed boxer is temporarily unconscious for a few seconds, he's not subject to further attack—as would be the case in an MMA contest—and can continue. How many times have we seen a fighter stagger to his feet and then get asked by the referee, "Do you want to continue?" Virtually every time the fighter will instinctively nod "yes," which of course exposes the fighter to additional brain trauma.

Even if boxing had the equivalent of the MMA "tap out" (see chapter six) under the circumstances just described, most boxers would still prefer to be carried out on their shield than be seen as quitters. That is the way of the gladiator, but it is also the way to irreversible brain damage. From 1993 to April 2019, seven deaths occurred in sanctioned MMA bouts and another nine MMA fighters reportedly died in unregulated bouts.[91] During that same period, over a hundred professional boxers died because of punishment incurred during a match, with all but two of the deaths attributed to brain trauma.[92] One might assume the higher number reflects greater boxing activity compared to MMA, but this is not the case. While exact numbers are difficult to pinpoint, there appear to be many more MMA bouts worldwide per year (including but not limited to those promoted by the UFC) than pro boxing bouts, especially since the early 2000s. This is yet another indication that boxing is the more dangerous sport.

In light of the above facts I believe that professional boxing should look to MMA for ideas to make boxing safer.

That isn't to say that boxing should morph into MMA, but rather that it should reduce the time boxers are exposed to punishment. Barring a knockout or submission, the longest MMA bout lasts twenty-five minutes for title fights and main events. Non-title fights last fifteen minutes.

Barring a knockout, the shortest length of a professional boxing match is twelve minutes (four three-minute rounds). Bouts scheduled for six, eight, ten, or twelve rounds go on for a total of eighteen to thirty-six minutes—again, barring a knockout. The statistics in chapter two show that there's a strong case to be made for limiting the number of scheduled rounds as an added safety measure. While the safest alternative is to limit professional fights to five three-minute rounds, there is still a place for six-, eight-, and ten-round bouts if the boxers are matched properly.

CHAPTER 15

Boxing Gloves: Saving the Hands at the Expense of the Brain

The hand was not made for punching. The hand was made for survival. That's why the hand has so many small bones, to grasp, to hold onto, to grab, to feel. It's not made to put blunt force against something solid.
—Teddy Atlas

For more than 150 years, professional prizefights were fought with bare fists (see chapter one). With the adoption of the Marquess of Queensberry rules in the late 19th century, pugilists were required to wear padded leather gloves (usually weighing five to eight ounces). Gloves were intended to make boxing appear less brutal and therefore more acceptable to the public and to elected officials, many of whom called for the abolition of boxing.

The Queensberry rules created the illusion that gloved boxing was safer than the bare-knuckle version. But it wasn't. Bare-knuckle fighters always worried about damaging their hands. They had to be careful where to place their punches and whether to throw with full force or not. Wearing gloves offered a layer of protection for the delicate bones of the hands, but far from making the sport safer, the gloved fist was a formidable clublike weapon. With less concern about damaging their hands, boxers were encouraged to throw innumerable full-force punches to an opponent's head, thereby increasing the likelihood of brain damage.

A LEGEND WEIGHS IN

In 1974 legendary movie actor James Cagney was interviewed by the *New York Times*'s sports columnist Red Smith. Cagney had been around boxing all his life and witnessed firsthand the damaging effects of the sport. Since he had doctors for brothers, he understood what happens to the brain when it is jarred repeatedly, as in a boxing match. Although Cagney can't be considered a boxing expert, his observations, both interesting and accurate, are worth noting. "Boxing gloves are actually a weapon, not a safety device," said Cagney:

> The glove does not protect the brain; it protects the hand. In fact, if you want to make boxing less dangerous, the best way would be to ban the boxing glove and any type of protection for the hand. I have been saying this for years. I worked with a lot of former fighters in the picture business,

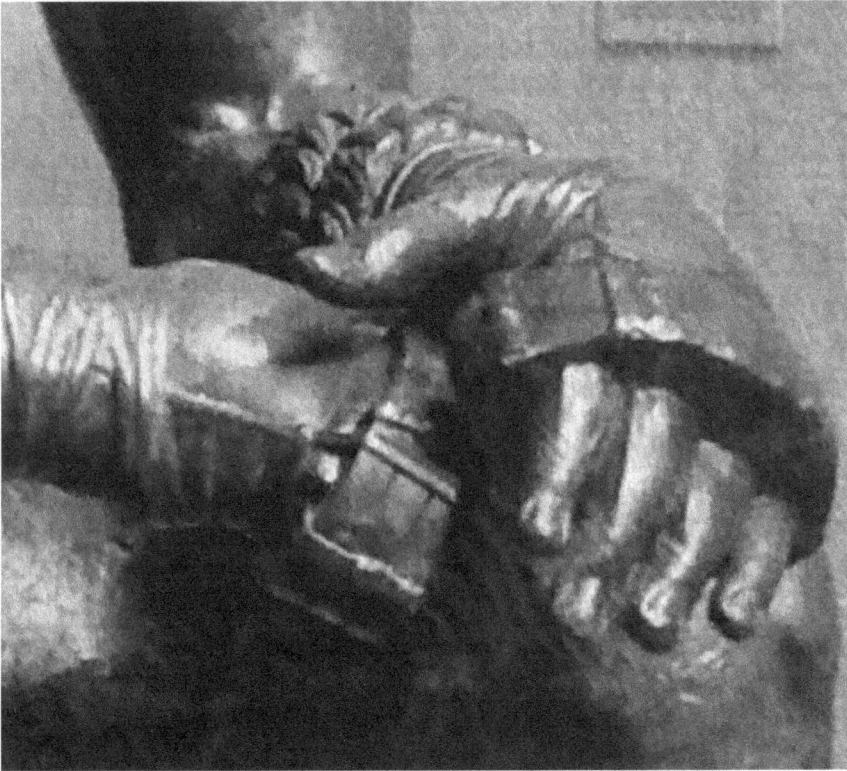

Boxing gloves in ancient Greece consisted of layers of leather straps covering the fists and forearms. *Photograph by Sol Korby*

and I saw the results of getting belted about the head. You know scar tissue once formed after a concussion continues to grow. That's why it's progressive encephalopathy [CTE]. If you ever hit anybody on top of the head with a bare fist, you wouldn't try it again. You would learn body-punching, and that's what I'm after. Gloves sacrifice the brain to preserve the metacarpals.[93]

Tony Gee, the foremost authority on the bare-knuckle era of boxing and author of the book *Up to Scratch: Bareknuckle Fighting and Heroes of the Prize-ring*, has done extensive research on the subject. He writes: "Pugilists who contested under both codes in the last decades of the 19th century tended to point out in interviews that they fought more to the body than the head in fights that they had with bare knuckles, given that there was not the protection for fragile hands which gloves gave."[94]

To offer further protection for their hands before putting on the gloves, boxers were permitted to wrap each hand in soft gauze that didn't exceed ten yards in length and two inches in width. The gauze was held in place by not more than four feet of surgeon's tape, one inch in width. This was standard for years, until 1985, when the amount of gauze was increased to thirteen yards for all weight divisions up to and including middleweight. For light heavyweight to heavyweight the amount of gauze allowed was twelve yards, held in place by eight feet of surgeon's tape for each hand. The bandages were evenly distributed across the hand. Currently, all fighters are allowed (for each hand) fifteen yards of soft gauze held in place by ten feet of surgeon's tape. This represents a substantial increase in the amount of allowable hand wraps over previous years. It appears that saving the hands at the expense of the brain is still a priority.

During boxing's Golden Age of talent and activity (the 1920s to 1950s), body punching was an integral part of an accomplished boxer's strategy. Today's boxers, by contrast, attempt few body punches per round. Instead, they aim most punches at an opponent's head. This isn't only because the extra tape and bandages offer greater protection to the hands. Like so many other techniques, the art of body punching is no longer taught. The last great body punchers were Roberto Duran and Julio Caesar Chavez. Sugar Ray Leonard was also adept at body punching, and Joe Frazier's vicious left hooks to an opponent's jaw were often preceded by several left hooks to the body.

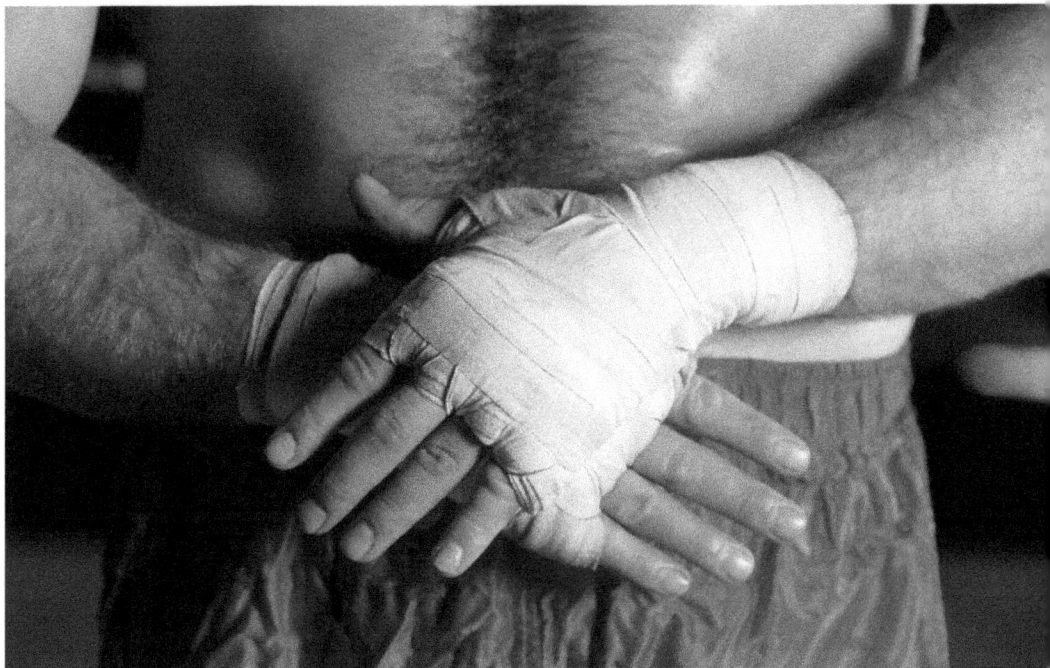

Modern boxers' hands are protected with several dozen feet of gauze and adhesive tape prior to their putting on eight- or ten-ounce gloves. *Action Plus Sports Images/Alamy Stock Photo*

John L. Sullivan, the last bare-knuckle heavyweight champion (1882–1892), appreciated the extra potency of a gloved punch to the jaw compared to one delivered with a bare fist. He used gloves during exhibitions with amateurs to ensure a knockout and at the same time protect his famous right fist. A few years after Jack Dempsey lost his heavyweight championship to Gene Tunney, in 1926, the ex-champ launched a comeback by barnstorming across the country fighting exhibitions against a slew of second-raters. He used 10-ounce gloves that kept his famous fists from being damaged while he racked up a string of quick knockouts.

BARE-KNUCKLE REDUX?

In 2018 an organization calling itself the Bare Knuckle Fighting Championships (BKFC) began promoting bare-knuckle boxing matches. In BKFC matches, fighters' wrists, mid-hands, and thumbs are taped, but the

If the lost art of body punching were revived, fewer punches would be aimed at the head. Tony Zale (right) and Rocky Graziano battle in 1948. *AP Images/ WideWorld*

knuckles are left exposed. Fights are limited to five two-minute rounds, but otherwise modern boxing rules apply.

Many of the competitors in today's bare-knuckle contests are MMA fighters, both active and retired, who are looking to rejuvenate their careers in a new combat sport. Only a few professional boxers have crossed over to the BKFC because any boxer who thinks he has a future in gloved boxing will not risk damaging his hands in a bare-knuckle match.

The bare-knuckle sport is gaining in popularity, though. A few years ago, only six state boxing commissions permitted bare-knuckle boxing, but the number is now up to twenty-five. In 2023 California legalized bare-knuckle boxing, but it remains illegal in Nevada and New York State.

Even though bare-knuckle bouts are limited to ten minutes of action, the damage involved can be severe. Injuries include broken noses, loosened teeth, lacerations, and extreme facial swelling. The brutality of the sport puts the BKFC in a position to grab a share of the lucrative MMA television market.

Are these modern-day bare-knuckle fighters at less risk of brain damage than their gloved-up counterparts? According to some studies, bare-knuckle boxing may be considered slightly safer than gloved boxing when it comes to brain damage. The available data suggests a lower concussion rate compared to gloved boxing, despite a higher rate of facial lacerations in bare-knuckle bouts. In one study three physicians with an interest in combat sports collected observational data from regulated bare-knuckle boxing events in six states from June 2018 through September 2020. Over this period, they recorded 131 bouts, all with a ringside physician present, involving 262 athletes. The doctor's observational study showed that 1.5 percent of bare-knuckle fighters exhibited concussion-like symptoms when examined by a ringside physician, compared to gloved boxers, with an estimated rate of 6 to 12 percent.

The doctors concluded that the most frequent injuries in bare-knuckle fights include lacerations and hand fractures, while concussions were uncommon compared to other injuries.[95] But again, it should be noted that bare-knuckle bouts can't surpass ten minutes of actual fighting, while gloved bouts range from twelve to thirty-six minutes. In addition, because it is easier to damage hands in a bare-knuckle bout, the number of punches thrown is less than in a traditional gloved contest.

DOES SIZE MATTER?

Since the boxing glove is essentially a weapon, research has focused on the size of the glove in relation to safety. Early studies recommended adopting the 10-ounce glove to reduce the hazard of brain injury resulting from high-peak accelerations delivered by blows to the head. A 1951 study done by the Cornell Aeronautical Lab for the New York State Athletic Commission concluded that the difference between 6- and 8-ounce gloves is not as great as between 6- and 10-ounce gloves. But powerful and damaging blows may be struck with any weight of glove.[96] Today 8-ounce gloves are the authorized weight for professional boxers weighing up to 147 pounds, and 10-ounce gloves for fighters who weigh more than that.

If bare-knuckle boxing would indeed cause less brain damage than the gloved variety, why not just ban gloves? That is easier said than done if you consider that gloved boxing has been around since the late 19th century. Established boxing traditions are not easily abandoned. Indeed, the change from bare knuckles to padded gloves took about twenty-five years to be fully accepted by most boxing fans. And the earliest gloves were nothing compared to the gloves boxers wear today, ranging in size from skintight (no thicker than driving gloves) to padded gloves weighing 2 to 5 ounces.

Consider the modern boxing glove. While much research has been done on the causes and effects of CTE, few studies have looked at the design and structure of the boxing glove. Except for weight, no uniform standards apply to the manufacture, quality, and construction of today's boxing gloves.

Most boxing glove manufacturers use layers of foam rubber and latex to fill the leather-covered gloves, while others use a mix of foam and horsehair. The density and firmness of the material varies. One popular brand that uses a combination of horsehair and a thin layer of foam is known for being a "puncher's glove" because heavy hitters believe it transmits more force than gloves from other manufacturers. Years ago, state boxing commissions insisted that boxers competing against each other wear the gloves made by the same manufacturer. Today, each boxer is allowed his choice of gloves from a list of approved manufacturers.

A BOXING GLOVE MANUFACTURER WEIGHS-IN

I decided to get a boxing glove manufacturer's take on the subject. Russ Anber is the CEO of Rival Boxing Gear, one of the industry's most successful boxing equipment manufacturers. His Canada-based company was started about twenty years ago. Before he started the business, Anber had already established a reputation as a fine trainer and cornerman.

Anber prides himself on the quality of his products. I asked what he thought about the lack of uniform standards for professional boxing gloves and whether the weight of the glove made a difference in terms of safety. Anber replied:

> I can't say whether a 6-ounce glove is safer than an 8- or 10- ounce glove. I'm not sure about that. We are talking about ounces. But what we are not talking about is the size or the dimension of the glove, or the thickness of the padding in the knuckle area. If we were to answer the question of how to make the glove safer, what should be required is a standardiza- tion of gloves regardless of the brand. Every state or country's boxing commission should come up with a way to say, "This is how the gloves must be made. That's it. There is no different way—no difference in

the thickness or padding." Some gloves have such little padding in the knuckle area and most of their weight is loaded in the wrist. But all the commissions care about is the weight of the glove—8 ounces or 10 ounces. That's all they care about. Put it on the scale and weigh it. Well, it shouldn't be that way. If you want to make a safer glove, do what amateur boxing does. Regardless of the brand that you use, USA Boxing [the national governing body that supervises amateur boxing in the United States] makes sure it is composed of the same layers, thickness, and foam that have been tested by USA Boxing and approved by them. That's what we need for professional boxing—a recipe for gloves that combines the best attributes of different manufacturer's gloves and puts them all together. That will give you a glove providing the best protection for both hands and face and holds up the longest, doesn't break down. So from then on this is the recipe you will use; this is how wide it has to be; this is how long it has to be; this is how thick the padding must be in the knuckle area. That's what we need to do.[97]

Although most people believe that a larger and heavier glove of at least 10 ounces is less damaging than a lighter one, studies show that it in fact causes more damage. In 1963, shortly after welterweight champion Benny "Kid" Paret was fatally injured in a nationally televised title match at Madison Square Garden, the New York State legislature investigated all aspects of professional boxing, producing a 198-page report. The legislative committee considered increasing the weight of gloves from 8 ounces to 12 ounces but with reservations:

In spite of the increased weight of the 12-ounce glove, which might serve to increase the force of the blow, the attendant increase in the size of the glove has two desirable effects. First, the force of the blow as it is delivered is spread over a greater portion of the body's surface resulting in the diminution of the punishing effect of the blow for the reason that fewer pounds' pressure per square inch of body surface are exerted. Secondly, the greater surface of the 12-ounce glove makes it more difficult to land a solid punch as each contestant has a greater area for defense against an oncoming blow. It appears as though a compromise is in order. The miracle of modern science should find it a relatively simple matter to incorporate the size of the 12-ounce glove with the weight of the 8-ounce glove.

Interestingly, the committee recommended "an experimental program of untaped hands of boxers in all boxing matches that will gradually bring about a more careful placing of punches, lessen the savagery of attack and develop more boxing skills."[98] Unfortunately, the experimental program never got off the ground. I'm sure managers, promoters, and boxers opposed it because they feared that allowing gloves but no tape would cause too many hand fractures. But the suggestion should perhaps be reconsidered, even though it would likely entail an adjustment period during which boxers would have to get used to fighting with just gloves and without the further protection of taped hands.

THE CALIFORNIA STUDY

In 1964 a survey conducted by the California State Athletic Commission came to its own conclusion about the safety of 10-ounce gloves:

> Both today's and former boxing champions, trainers and managers in the profession, medical men and manufacturers of boxing gloves have studied the problem extensively and all agree that the present 6- and 8-ounce size glove is preferable to the larger one because:
>
> (A)
> The larger 10-ounce glove tends to have a little less shock but the boxer will actually take more punishment because he will stay in the ring longer.
>
> (B)
> If a boxer is knocked out by the larger glove, the larger glove has a tendency to bruise more area.
>
> (C)
> In thirty-nine boxing contests the gloves have been weighed both before and after the bout. In all cases the gloves have weighed between 3 and 5 ounces more at the end of the contest [primarily due to an accumulation of sweat and water]. This added weight tends to make a boxer carry his hands lower. A punch with a heavier glove does more damage than one with a lighter glove.

The report included a statement by Max M. Novich, M.D., an orthopedic surgeon, boxing coach, and future president of the Association of Ringside

Physicians: "For one thing, I am going to suggest a lighter glove for contestants. The heavier the glove, the more lethal the blow. This may surprise the casual observer—but it's true."[99]

Even though these early boxing-glove investigations occurred at a time when gloves were filled with horsehair—foam- and latex-filled gloves weren't generally used until the 1980s—the results and conclusions shouldn't be discounted.

While there are no recent scientific studies of boxing gloves, the last one, from 1981, is worth looking at. Titled "Boxing Gloves Compared Using Dummy Head Acceleration Response" and conducted by the Wayne State University Department of Neurosurgery, it evaluated gloves from two manufacturers that had different materials and weights. The results are especially relevant because the study tested, among other gloves, one layered with foam rubber that resembled today's gloves. The study aimed to measure "the impact attenuation of various types of weights of boxing gloves used in professional matches and training fights." Gloves weighing 8, 10, 14, and 16 ounces were tested for their concussive effect.[100]

One manufacturer's 8-ounce glove—the one layered with foam rubber—significantly reduced concussive effect compared to another manufacturer's glove for the jab-to-moderate-blow range. But as the blow increased to knockout power, the concussive impact of the foam-filled glove was only slightly less than that of one filled with horsehair. The study also concluded that a 16-ounce training glove, along with adequate head protection, has desirable features for training. (This assumes the fighters in training do not try to knock each other out while sparring).[101]

The scientists who conducted the research admitted that the tests were not exhaustive but were "only a beginning to show what can be done. Part of the money going into the lucrative purses now common should be funneled back into research dedicated to fighter protection."[102]

The Wayne State University study also acknowledged a dilemma faced by those trying to decide which glove was safer:

The most important finding in this study is that gloves can be quantitatively evaluated relative to each other and to an absolute criterion based upon cerebral concussion. What is not immediately evident is what direction to take once possessed of this information. It would appear that if death due to brain injury is the problem in boxing, then the solution is to use the gloves which provide more cushion to a swing which lands. However, some argue for the glove that produces higher acceleration and consequently shorter fights with quick knockouts. They feel that the prolonged fights with many subconcussive blows are more damaging to the brain.[103]

The most recent research on the causes of CTE supports this view. The largest study to date of chronic traumatic encephalopathy appeared in the scientific journal *Nature Communications* in 2023. Using data collected on the donated brains of 631 former football players, it found that the cumulative force of subconcussive impacts—not diagnosed concussions—predicted future brain disease best.[104]

Would there be a place in boxing for a "safe" glove—if one could be invented—that absorbs most of the energy of a punch without jarring the head enough to cause a concussion?

The ideal use for a "safe" glove would be in a novice amateur boxer's early sparring sessions. An amateur boxer's first year in the gym is particularly difficult. The basic skills he or she will need require many months of practice and many rounds of sparring. During that time, the athlete gradually acquires the motor skills, conditioning, and muscle memory that eventually will help his body perform in the ring without conscious effort. A safe boxing glove used in sparring would allow the boxer to learn proper balance, timing, pacing, and how to land and avoid a variety of different punches while at the same time reducing, or even eliminating, the possibility of a concussion. At least the fighter will be better prepared to defend himself when the proverbial training wheels eventually come off and he is deemed ready for serious sparring that can lead to actual competition.

SUMMING UP

From the available studies and from comments from knowledgeable trainers and researchers, it appears that smaller gloves do reduce concussive effect—but it also depends on the content, size, and structure of the glove, and who is doing the punching.

In any case, a comprehensive study of the modern boxing glove and head guard to determine which design is safest is long overdue.

CHAPTER 16

Boxing's Parasites: How the Alphabet Organizations Undermine Boxing Safety

*The fight racket is an immense enterprise, governed by
corporations and supervised by accountants, and the commodity
for sale is the public suffering of young men. It was originally a fete
of the underworld, but now is the property of legitimate commerce.
No matter who runs the store, it still specializes in agony, humiliation,
and the possibility of deformity and insanity.*
—Jimmy Cannon

I n 1996 the noted author and journalist Pete Hamill, in an article for *Esquire* that decried the state of professional boxing, said this: "Every month, in this era of multimillion-dollar purses, of cable television and pay-per-view, prizefights are legally fixed through matchmaking. There are bogus champions in every weight division."

Hamill was an avid boxing fan for many years, until the incessant corruption that had plagued the sport for decades spiraled out of control in the 1990s and turned him off to the sport. He was also troubled by the life-altering brain damage that afflicted so many ex-boxers. But Hamill reserved his harshest criticism for the sleazy charlatans at the top of professional boxing's food chain, whose greed and arrogance had ruined the sport he once loved. He said: "You cannot love anything that lives in a sewer. And the world of boxing is more fetid and repugnant now than at any other time in its squalid history."[105]

More than a quarter-century later, those words still ring true. In fact, there are more bogus "world champions" in every weight division than ever before, and potentially life-threatening mismatches are still used to inflate the records of promising boxers or to protect a popular champion.

In the late 1970s professional boxing's lack of a national commissioner or unified international governing body opened the door to an alphabet soup of self-serving quasi-official sanctioning organizations. The WBC, WBA, IBF, and WBO all award title belts to champions recognized by their organization.[106] Their websites list the top fifteen title contenders for each weight division.

All four organizations are largely funded by sanctioning fees, typically 3 percent taken out of the total purse from both the champion and challenger, including pay-per-view earnings, broadcast earnings, and any other type of earning. Fees are capped at around $250,000 per fighter, which means that fighters who earn more than $10 million per fight will pay less than 3 percent of their purse unless they are fighting for more than one title.

The fees are paid in exchange for the fighters' opportunity to compete for a sanctioning organization's title belt.

The two oldest sanctioning organizations are headquartered in Mexico (WBC) and Panama (WBA). Both are notoriously vague when it comes to their finances. "They collect percentages of a fighter's purse in sanctioning fees every time he fights," Joseph Spinelli, a former FBI agent who investigated bribery in boxing, once told the *New York Times*. "No one knows where it goes or who it goes to. They're not accountable to anyone.[107]

The WBC, WBA, IBF, and WBO (the Alphabet organizations), maintain mutually beneficial relationships with boxing's dominant promoters. When a promoter wants to make sure that a popular champion under his control is granted an easy title defense, the sanctioning organization cooperates by moving an inferior opponent into its list of top-ten challengers. A challenger's rating with a sanctioning organization lends a kind of legitimacy to a title fight, which makes it easier for a promoter to sell the fight to media. But even casual boxing fans know that the monthly ratings of the sanctioning organizations can't be trusted.

"In baseball, the standings reflect a quantifiable reality," wrote investigative journalist Jack Newfield in 2002. "In boxing, the ratings (which supposedly rank fighters according to ability, from one to ten with a number-one ranking guaranteeing a lucrative fight for the title) are at best impressionistic and at worst totally corrupt—sold for cash."

He added: "Everyone in boxing knows that the sanctioning bodies have no legitimacy. They force champions to pay huge fees for the right to defend their titles. They strip champions of their titles if they don't go along with the sport's backroom politics. They assign incompetent judges to fights. They are more like bandits than regulators."

Newfield explained the difference between the way the hoods fixed fights in the 1950s and how the sanctioning organizations accomplish the same result using a less direct approach. He wrote:

"A gangster doesn't strut into the dressing room, a cigar in his teeth, and whisper to the fighter, 'Tonight isn't your night, kid. You're going down in the sixth.' The corruption now is more subtle, sophisticated, and systemic. It depends more on fixing the rankings than fixing the fights."[108]

Nothing has changed in the twenty-odd years since Newfield's article. In 2021 public filings and court documents revealed that a Florida-based company named Sports Consulting Services (SCS) had acted as the go-between for the WBA in soliciting bribes from promoters in return for getting their fighters onto the WBA's top-ten contender list. The documents also indicated that SCS was controlled or managed by individuals employed by or closely associated with the World Boxing Association.[109] The reaction of the boxing world to this recent scandal was muted. The industry is so used to this type of corruption that no one paid much attention.

In a June 2023 editorial, Matt Christie, editor of England's venerable *Boxing News*, lambasted the sanctioning organizations and their nefarious connection to the sport's major promoters:

If you haven't looked for a while, take a nose at the rankings these gangs produce every month and ask yourself why they're all so different when they're all supposedly following the same results and form. In nearly every division, each sanctioning body will highly rank a little-known fighter who is unranked by their rival organizations. Imagine some randomer who hadn't won a match at a decent level suddenly being ranked as the third best tennis player on the planet simply because their manager was in cahoots with the head of the sport. The equivalent happens in boxing all of the time and nobody even blinks. . . . Anyone who has followed boxing for any length of time will know that having four sanctioning bodies in existence causes chaos. The boxers know it. The broadcasters know it. The promoters know it. The media know it. Yet they all keep the sanctioning bodies in business by facilitating their policies, rankings, and belts.[110]

Philadelphia boxing promoter J. Russell Peltz, who singlehandedly revived boxing in that city from the 1970s to the early 2000s, is currently a consultant guiding the careers of several young boxers. Peltz laments the destructive effect the sanctioning bodies have had on professional boxing's integrity and cohesion, especially since the 1990s: "Imagine if there were no playoffs in baseball and every division winner—the National League East or American League West—went around claiming to be the world champion. If they never play each other they'd all say 'We are the world champions.' That is what the sanctioning bodies have done. It's outrageous and their rankings are just so bogus."

Because he's been immersed in boxing since 1969, nothing surprises Peltz, certainly not the pervasive corruption that still plagues the sport.

Peltz continued: "I went to one of [the Alphabets'] conventions years ago in Florida. I'm not going to say which one. I sat down with another promoter and the ratings chairman of that sanctioning body. The promoter was a friend of mine. I saw him give the ratings chairman a list of four of his fighters and he said, 'I think these guys should all be rated' and *presto* the next month they were all rated in the top ten. Now what that promoter did for that ratings committee guy when I wasn't around I don't know. But I know that guys today are buying rankings. I know it. Was I there when money passed? No. But I know at least one of the organizations, and maybe two, has a bagman who takes money to put guys in the rankings."[111]

LETHAL CONSEQUENCES

A rating not based on merit can have lethal consequences for the boxer. An overmatched tennis player can walk away from a loss with nothing more serious than a bruised ego, but in professional boxing, the stakes are much higher. The policies of the sanctioning organizations can result in serious injury, or worse. The pay-for-play scam that Russell Peltz described began in the late 1970s. Sooner or later the deception was going to end in tragedy.

It turned out to be sooner.

On November 13, 1982, a South Korean fighter named Duk Koo Kim was knocked out by the WBA lightweight champion Ray "Boom Boom"

In 1982 WBA lightweight champion Ray Mancini knocked out Duk Koo Kim in the 14th round. Kim died five days later, after emergency brain surgery, a victim of boxing's corrupt rating system. *AP Photo/Jeff Scheid*

Mancini in the fourteenth round of a title fight in a parking-lot stadium built outside Caesars Palace in Las Vegas. Before leaving the ring Kim collapsed and became unconscious. Diagnosed with a subdural hematoma, he died five days after undergoing emergency brain surgery. The fight was nationally televised on CBS-TV.

The following month, in response to the tragedy, the WBC announced that, in the interest of boxing safety, all WBC title fights would be shortened from fifteen to twelve rounds. The WBA, not wanting to appear uninterested in safety, agreed to do the same. The era of fifteen-round title bouts came to an end.

SMOKE SCREEN

The WBC's decision to limit their title fights to twelve rounds appeared designed to enhance safety, which it might have done—if that was its actual intention. But the organization's true purpose was to use the tragedy to create a smoke screen and divert attention away from the real source of the problem—an unreliable and easily corrupted rating system that too often allowed mismatches in title fights. According to the rules of the Alphabet organizations, only a rated contender can be granted a title bout. Of course, the public is not privy to the back-room chicanery that grants an inferior fighter a top-ten rating by these organizations.

The tragic outcome of the Kim–Mancini bout put this entire corrupt system under a spotlight—for a time.

Mismatches in title fights have occurred throughout boxing history, but not nearly to the extent of what we've seen since the promoter and Alphabet cartels took control of the sport over forty years ago. Before the fight, Duk Koo Kim was an obscure South Korean boxer with an undistinguished 17-1-1 record. Seven of his opponents had never had a professional fight. Six others had seven or fewer fights. There was nothing in Kim's record to justify a title fight. Nevertheless, the WBA named him their number-one lightweight contender to give Mancini, a popular champion, an easy televised win.

Kim surprised everyone with his stubborn resistance. Every time Mancini hurt him, Kim fought back furiously. But despite holding his own for the first ten rounds he was taking a vicious beating, especially from the eleventh to fourteenth rounds. Kim might have survived had the bout been limited to eight or ten rounds.

If the WBC were truly interested in safety, it would not just have shortened title fights to twelve rounds; it would have stopped sanctioning dangerously flawed fights. Just ten months after Kim–Mancini, a fighter was fatally injured in the twelfth round of a twelve-round WBC title bout. On September 1, 1983, Kiko Bejines and Alberto Davila fought for the "WBC Interim World Bantamweight" title in Los Angeles. Why was Bejines granted a title fight? He had not fought in thirteen months before, and he lost that fight by TKO. Among his thirty-four previous opponents there were only a few recognizable names. But in a move comparable to the skulduggery that propelled Duk Koo Kim to contender status, Kiko Bejines was given a top-ten rating in the WBC's list of bantamweight contenders. Meanwhile, Alberto Davila was a legitimate contender and an experienced veteran who had already faced a dozen world-class boxers in fifty-three bouts.

In a hard fought and punishing contest, Bejines was competitive for the first ten rounds but became increasingly fatigued. Davila attacked furiously at the start of the twelfth round and floored Bejines, who lost consciousness moments after being counted out. Taken by ambulance to a hospital, he underwent emergency brain surgery but died three days later, just short of his twenty-first birthday.

Ironically, instead of making boxing less dangerous, the twelve-round distance has made boxing less safe. This was not because championship fights were now three rounds shorter—that was a good thing. The problem was that over the next decade, the Alphabet organizations, in order to generate additional sanctioning fees, created seven new weight divisions (with each organization crowning its own world champion). As a result, the number of twelve-round title fights multiplied rapidly (as did the sanctioning fees). Many of these bouts would end badly for unqualified and overmatched challengers who would've never gotten a title shot in the pre-Alphabet era.

Eager to milk the sport, the Alphabets were just getting started. According to the WBC guidelines, promoters must pay an annual registration fee in the $7,000 range. What's more, they must pay between $5,000 and $25,000 for every fight, depending on the type of title and weight category. This promoter fee is in addition to the sanctioning fees paid by the fighters.

Limited to one champion for each weight division, the Alphabets sought other creative ways to increase sanctioning fees. Adding more weight divisions—it was already up to seventeen from the original eight—would be too hard a sell. To circumvent this roadblock, the WBC came up with a clever innovation that the other Alphabet organizations quickly copied. What the WBC did was multiply the number of belt-holders by inventing additional titles *within* each of the seventeen weight categories. The new titles were named "International," "Global," "Pan Pacific," "Interim," "Continental," "Super," "Super, Super," "Regular," "Green," "Diamond," "Gold," "Silver," "Oceana," "Francophone," "Fedelatin," "Champion in Recess," "Franchise." All required a sanctioning fee from both challenger and champion for the privilege of fighting for a "title." Even pro wrestling wouldn't have had the nerve to create this many specious "champions."

The sanctioning organizations also began charging fees for bouts designated as a "title eliminator," in which the winner supposedly earns the right to challenge the champion. This was yet another ruse that allowed the Alphabets to extort more blood money from fighters even though no title

The WBC, WBA, IBF, and WBO have saturated the sport with hundreds of belt holders, thereby diluting the significance of the words "world champion."

would be at stake. Since the winner is not actually *guaranteed* a title opportunity, any fight can be labeled an "eliminator."

These unprecedented changes to professional boxing's traditional infrastructure demonstrated the sport's need for a legitimate centralized regulatory body, but none emerged. The WBC, WBA, IBF, and WBO continued to recognize their own set of champions and top-ten contenders for each of the seventeen weight divisions. (The WBA alone has forty-five so-called "champions" holding various titles.)

For the most part relations between the four sanctioning organizations remain fractious. Each Alphabet refuses to list champions recognized by a rival group in their ratings of top-ten challengers, even if a fighter is the toughest opponent their own champion can face. Because the disparate ratings of the four groups are never consolidated, a thin talent pool gets stretched even thinner. Take, for example, the middleweight division's ratings for January 2024: Of the forty top-ten contenders rated by the WBC, WBA, IBF, and WBO, only seven names appear on all four lists. All other weight classifications are like that.

Under these conditions, it is difficult for promoters and fans to accurately assess the quality of the hundreds of rated contenders. Adding to the uncertainty, many of the rated fighters have been carefully navigated to undefeated records by being put into fights where they knock over third-rate opposition.

THE ALPHABETS AND BOXING SAFETY

In 2020, before the pandemic slowed the pace, the WBC, WBA, IBF, and WBO sanctioned nearly two hundred title fights, with most scheduled for twelve rounds. The previous twenty years had seen similar numbers. By contrast, from the 1920s to the 1960s, there were between thirty-two and forty title fights annually.[112]

It is the proliferation of hundreds of twelve-round title fights matching inexperienced boxers with poor defensive skills that has made the sport more dangerous. In decades past these fighters would still be learning their trade, gradually gaining experience in bouts scheduled for six or eight rounds. The rare fifteen-round title shot would be several years away.

A KEY ISSUE

In the years since the twelve-round limit became standard, dozens of professional fighters have died from punishment received in bouts that ended in either the tenth, eleventh, or twelfth round. More fighters have died in those rounds than in previous decades because over the past forty years so many unqualified, inexperienced and mismatched boxers have taken part in twelve-round bouts. As noted in chapter two, from 1980 to 2023, sixty-four boxers died in these bouts. At the same time, thirty-six boxers were fatally injured in rounds one to five. Of that number twenty-nine fights ended in rounds one to four, and seven ended in round five.

But for the thousands of fighters who survive their careers, the key issue is brain trauma that leads to symptoms of CTE and eventual dementia. So shortening fights—including, of course, the absurd number of twelve-round Alphabet title bouts—won't only save lives, it will benefit all boxers. Yet the WBC—like the other three major sanctioning organizations—has never called for the elimination of twelve-round fights.

BUSINESS AS USUAL

Forty years after Duk Koo Kim was beaten to death in front of a live TV audience, it's still business as usual in boxing. Consider the November 5, 2022, WBA super-middleweight title fight pitting the champion, David Morrell, against Aidos Yerbossynuly of Kazakhstan. After four years as a pro, Morrell, a former Cuban national amateur star, has become one of the world's elite fighters. He defended his title in Minneapolis in a fight broadcast by Showtime, which had an exclusive contract with Morell's promoter at that time.

Even though Yerbossynuly hadn't fought in fourteen months, the WBA named him the mandatory challenger. This should have raised a red flag for the Minnesota Boxing Commission, at least to the point where they warned the referee and ringside doctors to watch the challenger closely.

From the beginning of the fight, it was clear that Yerbossynuly was in over his head. Up to the knockout, in the final moments of the twelfth round, the "mandatory challenger" hadn't won a single round. The number of head punches he took round after round alarmed even the television commentators, who questioned why the referee had allowed the fight to continue past the seventh round. (According to CompuBox numbers, Morell landed 237 punches, compared to just eighty for his opponent.)

The boxing establishment continues to sanction dangerous mismatches. In 2022 WBA champion David Morrell knocked out Aidos Yerbossynuly, and the challenger survived emergency brain surgery. *Photograph by Esther Lin*

The referee and the ringside physician, seemingly oblivious to the one-sided beatdown, let it continue. A few seconds after the referee finally stopped the fight, in the twelfth round, Yerbossynuly collapsed. Rushed to a hospital, the unconscious boxer underwent emergency brain surgery to remove an intracranial blood clot. Seventeen days later, he came out of a medically induced coma and was said to be showing signs of improvement. He is lucky to be alive—no thanks to the incompetent referee, doctors, and commission personnel. And, of course, the WBA.

• • •

Another example: On February 27, 2021, Saul "Canelo" Alvarez of Mexico defended his WBA Super World Super Middleweight title against Avni Yildirim of Turkey in a bout that took place in Miami. Also at stake was the vacant WBC World Super Middleweight title. Yildirim was unrated, had never defeated a name opponent, and hadn't fought in two years. Nevertheless, the Mexico City–based WBC catapulted him to its number-one super middleweight slot, which permitted the sanction and guaranteed an easy win for Alvarez.

The phony rating didn't fool Vegas oddsmakers. Yildrim entered the ring a 12-1 underdog, but the odds might as well have been 100-1. Alvarez's record was 54-1-2 compared to Yildrim's relatively thin 21-2. The over-matched challenger was outclassed and outpunched from the opening bell of a fight that resembled a sparring match between an experienced pro and a beginner. The hopelessly outclassed Yildirim barely threw a punch, while Alvarez's powerful body punches broke the challenger down early. The inept Yildrim refused to continue when the bell rang to start the fourth round. It was a sad performance by the WBC's number-one super middleweight contender, but at least he knew when to quit.

Both fights raise important questions: Did anyone at Minnesota's Office of Combative Sports (a division of the Minnesota Department of Labor and Industry), or anyone at the Florida Boxing Commission wonder about the ranking of Yerbossynuly and Yildrim? Were the commissioners even aware of the WBA's and WBC's history of issuing questionable ratings? If they didn't know, why do they hold positions of responsibility in the sport? And if they did know, don't their actions make them complicit in endangering fighters' lives?

• • •

These fights aren't exceptions. The sanctioning organizations have approved hundreds of twelve-round title fights that matched a superior fighter against a top-ten contender whose record didn't justify his rating. From 1999 to 2022 nineteen boxers were fatally injured in title bouts. Fourteen of those bouts were sanctioned by the WBC, IBF, and WBO (see chapter seventeen). Significantly, only one of the fourteen fights ended before the tenth round.[113] This is yet another indication that shorter fights would create a safer environment for the boxers.

FROM EVOLUTION TO DEVOLUTION

It isn't uncommon today for a boxer to win a title with less than a dozen professional fights on his résumé. While many such boxers possess sterling amateur credentials, they don't get the experience they need to refine and expand their skills in the pro ranks. This includes learning how to properly pace themselves for bouts that go beyond three rounds and adjust their style to different circumstances. These skills are hard to learn because today's pro boxers rarely fight more than three or four times a year. Subjecting the body and psyche of a novice professional to a punishing ten- or twelve-round contest—as often happens today—is dangerous and unproductive. A few fighters can be fast-tracked, but they're the exception.

In previous decades boxers had to earn a title fight by defeating legitimately ranked contenders. And after winning a title, the new champion had to defend it against other good fighters. It was a natural-selection process in which—more often than not—the best fighters fought each other. But this process is gone from the boxing landscape. When natural selection disappeared from boxing, it also eliminated evolution, and that is what the present system does. It partly explains why most of today's champions and contenders appear so mediocre compared to the experienced artists of the Golden Age.

Unfortunately, over the past twenty-five years, boxing commissions in various countries have imitated the four major sanctioning organizations. They have endangered the health of boxers by allowing far too many ten- or twelve-round regional "championship" contests that should be relegated to preliminary status.

So far only one director of an Alphabet sanctioning organization has served jail time for activities related to fixing the ratings. On February 14,

2001, Robert W. Lee Sr., founder and former president of the International Boxing Federation, which was based in New Jersey at the time, was found guilty of racketeering, money laundering, and tax evasion and sentenced to twenty-two months in prison. Prosecutors argued that Lee accepted bribes over fifteen years in exchange for awarding rankings that gave boxers a chance at lucrative IBF title fights.[114]

"THE RED-LIGHT DISTRICT OF SPORTS"

Professional boxing was accurately characterized by columnist Jimmy Cannon as "the Red-Light District of Sports." Throughout its history, professional boxing has never been free of corruption and exploitation. The mobsters of the 1950s TV era controlled the careers of many champions and contenders. Fixed fights were arranged to create betting coups. Boxers who refused Mob management didn't get lucrative television bouts.

There were other abuses during the pre-Alphabet era. In the 1930s and 1940s great Black boxers like Jack McVey, Harry Smith, Holman Williams, Charley Burley, Lloyd Marshall, Jimmy Bivins, Cocoa Kid, and Eddie Booker never got to fight for a championship. Archie Moore was a top-rated contender for ten years before he got a title shot, in 1952. Once having won the light-heavyweight title, Moore, one of the sport's all-time greats, held onto it for the next eight years. But despite its imperfections, boxing kept a reliable and honest rating system in an infrastructure that allowed for the orderly succession of eight champions in eight weight divisions.

While there's no question that boxing was damaged by Mob influence in the 1950s, the damage was not institutionalized—in other words, it was reparable.

In 1961 boxing's underworld czars, notably Frankie Carbo and Frank "Blinky" Palermo, were sentenced to lengthy prison terms after being convicted of conspiracy and extortion. But within a decade and a half, a new Mob had taken over the sport with the rise of promoter-Alphabet cartels. The cartels' arrival quickly led to the balkanization of professional boxing, which effectively put an end to a system that—albeit imperfect—at least encouraged competitive matches between legitimately ranked contenders. Sadly, four decades later, the present system has become so institutionalized it may be impossible to change it.

Author Jim Brady put the title situation in historical perspective in his book *Boxing Confidential: Power, Corruption and the Richest Prize in Sport*:

In the 1950s, there were approximately five thousand fighters world-wide. There were generally eight weight divisions, with one champion in each. That breaks down to one champ every 625 boxers. Today, with just the major sanctioning bodies and not counting the whackos, you have about one 'world champion' for every sixty-nine pros. It's ridiculous. Championship belts used to mean something. Now all they're good for is holding up your pants.[115]

If boxing were run like other major professional sports, the sanctioning organizations' actions would have gotten them banned long ago. Author and historian Springs Toledo accurately assessed the damage done to the sport by the unholy alliance of unscrupulous promoters and corrupt sanctioning organizations in his book *The Gods of War.*

Rich, fat, and easy to identify, today's profiteers come in assorted colors and are doing what any self-respecting hoodlum from the 1950s would consider perverse: They're killing the sport. Unchecked promot-ers turn their backs on public demand for matchups unless they have options on both corners. So-called sanctioning bodies create unnecessary weight divisions and spawn sham titles to expand their influence and col-lect more fees. It's enough to wax nostalgic about the less-bad old days when Frankie Carbo was fixing fights in the shadow of Madison Square Garden. . . . The sanctioning organizations are defecating on the once-regal concept of champion.[116]

You have only to look at the following statistics to realize how outrageous the devaluation of titles has become: In the thirty years between 1950 and 1980, there were 186 world champions; in the *twenty* years between 2000 and 2021, there have been 1,128—a staggering 500 percent increase.[117]

Whereas the old hoods of the fifties were careful to stay in the shadows, today's crooks have no such qualms. In fact, the boxing industry, to its ever-lasting shame, honors and pays homage to the likes of Don King and Jose Sulaiman, the self-proclaimed president for life of the WBC, both of whom have been inducted into the International Boxing Hall of Fame.

The day after King was inducted into the hall, in 1997, *New York Post* sports columnist Wallace Matthews expressed his disgust with the choice in these words:

Why honor a man who has brought little but dishonor to a sport and its participants? . . . . King has given boxing much of the bad name it has today with advertisers and the public. Enshrining a Don King with the likes of Sugar Ray Robinson, Muhammad Ali, Joe Louis and Jack Dempsey is the same as inducting into Cooperstown the gangsters who fixed the 1919 World Series. Or inducting into the Basketball Hall of Fame the creeps behind the CCNY and Boston College point-shaving scandals. It is as bad as an Italian-American Hall of Fame inducting Al Capone.

Matthews continued with a partial litany of King's criminality:

He forced Muhammad Ali into a fight with Larry Holmes when he knew Ali was suffering from brain damage, and he once threatened to break Larry Holmes's kneecaps [when Holmes, after discovering King was ripping him off, expressed a desire to fight for another promoter], and he found ways to cut a $1.9 million purse from Tim Witherspoon down to $90,000. He refused to let Frankie Randall accept a $4 million offer to fight Pernell Whitaker and made him fight a rematch with Julio Cesar Chavez for a fraction of the money, and then he made sure his buddies in the WBC stole the fight away from him. [Ed] Brophy [the executive director of the IBHOF] might as well induct Frankie Carbo and Blinky Parlermo who were undoubtedly as influential a part of the boxing community in their time as King is in his.

The same year King was elected, Sugar Ray Leonard and Jose Torres, great champions, were also elected, about which Matthews added that Leonard and Torres "belong in the Hall of Fame. Don King does not, and his very presence in the same building with those two changes the entire character of the place. Now it is just another Hall of Shame."[118]

THE WAY IT WAS—AND WILL NEVER BE AGAIN

In an industry that has often been tarnished by its association with criminals, the one saving grace has always been the boxers, without whom there would be no sport. Although every era has produced its share of great fighters, in terms of the depth of talent, level of activity, and media coverage, the 1920s to the 1950s was a Golden Age for the sport. When a champion retired or moved up to another weight division a tournament was usually organized to fill the vacancy and crown his successor. Only two organizations rated boxers—the National Boxing Association and *The Ring* magazine. The NBA, begun in 1921, was comprised of a loose confederation of forty-three state boxing commissions. In 1924 *The Ring* magazine, under the leadership of Nat Fleischer, also began rating boxers. Though *The Ring's* ratings carried more weight, both the NBA and Fleischer were trusted by the boxing community to be impartial. As a measure of their accuracy—but more important their veracity—both organizations' ratings were almost always identical. During his years leading *The Ring*, Fleischer was boxing's unofficial commissioner and, in a sense, the sport's conscience. Boxing started its decline in popularity and activity in the mid-1950s, but the Golden Age that began in the early 1920s could be said to have officially ended with Fleischer's passing, in 1972.

The NBA sanctioned world champions as did the once powerful and respected New York State Athletic Commission. (During the Golden Age New York City was the epicenter of the sport.) The world champions recognized by each were usually identical, though occasional disputes arose. But these disputes were most often quickly resolved by matching the NBA and NYSAC champions. (When a title was split, the British and European boxing authorities usually went along with the New York State Athletic Commission.)

The NBA did have a "sanctioning fee"—it was a token *one dollar* (yes, one dollar), and the promoter paid it. The NBA's ratings were determined by fewer than a dozen unpaid volunteers, but they knew boxing, and they also shared a love and respect for the sport. Exploiting professional boxing to make money wasn't their goal. It's worth noting that from the 1920s to the 1960s the top-ten contender ratings of the NBA and *The Ring* were never tampered with, paid for, or otherwise compromised. Their only purpose was to add a measure of credibility and coherence to boxing, things that are sadly lacking today.

Many fans old enough to have seen the heyday of Ali, Frazier, Foster, Monzon, Hagler, Duran, Leonard, Hearns, Arguello, and Pryor no longer follow the sport. If not for the interest of younger fans in the twenty-to-forty age range, the sport would have lost much of its audience. Unless they're familiar with the history, however, today's fans think multiple champions for seventeen weight divisions and twelve-bout pros with three or four title belts is the way it has always been.

BLOOD MONEY

By the early 2000s the WBC had collected over $20 million in sanctioning fees from boxers' purses, of which an estimated 90 percent were generated in the United States.[119] Over the past forty years, despite the millions they've collected, the Alphabet organizations have contributed nothing of value to the sport. Their major contribution? To generate unprecedented confusion and disappointment and to cause many fans to become fed up with the sport.

The rank-and-file boxer still has no union, pension plan, or health benefits. Yet few boxers have complained or questioned why they must turn over a huge chunk of their hard-earned money to the sanctioning bodies. The boxers know who's in control, and they aren't about to risk their careers and future paydays by rocking the boat.

Former heavyweight champion Evander Holyfield paid about $600,000 dollars in fees to the sanctioning organizations during his career. When asked what they did with all that money, Holyfield replied, "I can't recall them doing anything but showing up and having judges to judge the fight."[120]

The most lucrative cash cow for promoter Don King and WBC president Jose Sulaiman was Mike Tyson. King was Tyson's promoter and a close associate of Sulaiman. The relationship between King and Sulaiman can be accurately described as a partnership in which the WBC president was a subservient junior partner to King rather than an independent regulator. Often it was King who told Sulaiman which judges or referee to assign to his shows. Who can forget the night Buster Douglas, a 40-to-1 underdog, pulled off boxing's greatest upset by knocking out Mike Tyson to win the title. King, upset that his money machine had lost, claimed that Douglas had been given a long count by the referee after being knocked down. Minutes after Douglas was crowned champion, King ordered Sulaiman to strip him of the WBC belt and return the title to Tyson. Dutifully following the orders of his boss, Sulaiman made the announcement, but the outcry from the media and the public was such that King was forced to concede and reversed his decision the following day.

For just three title fights Tyson was charged an astounding $1,050,000 in fees, and at least once, King ordered Tyson to pay Sulaiman sanctioning fees that exceeded the scheduled amount.

Before he became involved with professional boxing, Don King had been a Cleveland, Ohio, numbers racketeer. Released from prison in 1971, after serving four years on a manslaughter conviction, he entered pro boxing as a manager, and by 1975 he had become one of the sport's dominant promoters.

In 1989, Tyson signed a contract with King that effectively gave the promoter complete control of the fighter's career. Within a year, Tyson lost the heavyweight championship to Buster Douglas. In 1992, Tyson was convicted of rape and spent the next three years in prison. After his release, he launched a comeback but showed extremely poor judgment by returning to King. Over the next two years, he won and lost a portion of the heavyweight championship while earning tens of millions of dollars. Tyson's relationship with King ended in 1998, when Tyson found out that his money was gone and sued King for $100 million, alleging that the promoter had cheated him out of millions over more than a decade. Aside from what King had stolen out of his fight purses, additional millions were billed to Tyson in the form of sanctioning fees that Sulaiman then shared with his de facto boss King. In an out-of-court settlement, Tyson received $14 million.

DISTORTING THE HISTORICAL RECORD

In addition to their other misdeeds, the sanctioning organizations also distort boxing's rich history. By creating so many fake championships, they have obscured how hard it was to become a top contender, let alone win a title, back when there were only eight weight classes and eight world champions.

In the eighty-eight years from 1892 to 1980, only four fighters won titles in three weight divisions: Bob Fitzimmons, Tony Canzoneri, Barney Ross, and Henry Armstrong—all bona fide greats. Over the next forty-one years (1981–2022) forty-eight fighters achieved that same feat. In fact, twenty of them won titles in between four and eight of the seventeen weight divisions.[121]

A THEATER OF THE ABSURD

The saturation point may still not have been reached when it comes to the creation of even more title belts and weight classes to generate additional fees for these hustlers and their sycophants.

In 2020 Mauricio Sulaiman, the WBC's "President for Life"—a title inherited from his father, Jose—announced the creation of the "bridgerweight" division, which exists between the WBC's cruiserweight and heavyweight divisions and is meant for fighters weighing between 191 and 224 pounds. When one considers the decline of boxing skills over the past several decades, and the unprecedented number of heavyweights in the 230- to 270-pound range, all things being equal, there is a valid argument to be made for this new division, even if its creation was likely influenced by financial incentives. But the addition of yet another weight classification brought the total number of weight divisions to eighteen—almost double the number from the 1920s to the 1950s. Boxing already suffers from an overabundance of titles. It is past time to decrease the number of superfluous weight divisions. At least five should be eliminated—especially in the 108- to 140-pound categories—where the difference between weight divisions is only three or four pounds.

The WBC's annual convention in 2023 took place in Tashkent, Uzbekistan (of all places). In addition to the self-congratulatory videos and awards, the convention featured several presentations intended to show how much the WBC cared about boxing safety. One presentation involved a cell-phone application called BoxMed that "will collect data on fighters and create a central database for the sport." The app will also be used for weight management of fighters. A year later, the specifics of how the WBC will implement and enforce the app remain vague.

Meanwhile, the sanctioning body has had little to say on a crucial topic that touches directly on fighters' health and safety—the poor performance and lack of accountability of referees who wait too long to stop a fight. The WBC has avoided the topic because it would be seen as interfering with the relationship between promoters and certain favored referees. It would also bring unwanted attention to the WBC's policy of barring any referee, no matter how competent, from working any of their fights if he has refereed bouts for a rival organization. So much for making safety a priority.

The second session of the day featured a speaker introduced as the WBC's "chairman of the recently created 'Mismatches Committee.'" Considering the huge number of mismatches approved by the WBC over the past forty years such a committee was, and still is, urgently needed and long overdue. But it's hard to take this new committee seriously, as long as the organization acquiesces to the demands of promoters and continues to sanction fights based on a flawed and dishonest rating system. If the promoter wants a fight to happen—mismatch or not—the WBC will not object. This conflict of interest will assure that mismatches will continue. It's telling to note that one year after the "mismatch committee" was announced, there is still no mention of it on the WBC's website.

This is not to say that the WBC is completely unconcerned about boxing safety. They are, to the extent that it improves their image. But their grand pronouncements of safety-related innovations, while making for good PR, are always in the "discussion" or "planning stage." This is in addition to the WBC's habit of taking credit for long-established rule changes, such as the four-roped ring (instituted by the California Athletic Commission in the mid-1960s) and day-before weigh-ins (instituted by the Nevada Commission in the 1980s). The only significant rule change that can truthfully be claimed by the sanctioning body is the 1983 rule reducing title fights from fifteen to twelve rounds. But the safety benefit of that policy change has been undermined by the WBC's frenzied collection of additional fees by sanctioning hundreds of twelve-round fights each year, many of which unnecessarily endanger fighters.

In chapter seventeen I analyze fourteen fatalities that occurred in fights sanctioned by the WBC, IBF, and WBO. The fights took place from 1995 to 2022 and represent nearly 12 percent of the 119 boxing-related deaths that occurred during that time. Eight were sanctioned by the WBC, five by the IBF, and one by the WBO. Twelve of the fourteen fights were scheduled for twelve rounds, and two for ten rounds. Significantly, thirteen ended between the tenth and twelfth rounds.

While they haven't done much to protect fighters' health, there is one thing that the WBC does better than any of the other Alphabet organizations. It has perfected the art of virtue signaling— projecting the appearance of being socially responsible and innovative—while never following through. The WBC has been adept at using buzzwords and slick videos filled with exaggerations and lies to create an illusion of progress.

Their main priority isn't safety, of course; it's staying in power and making money. The dollars tossed to a few brain-damaged ex-champions or contributed to a medical facility that is researching CTE, provides good PR, but it doesn't do anything to *prevent* brain damage. If a major promoter insists on a fight, the Alphabets will sanction it.

Clearly the sanctioning organizations need to disappear, and all it would take is for every state and national boxing commission to ban sanctioning fees. But blocking effective reforms like this are dominant promoters and powerful media entities. Like a gang of outlaws who have taken over a Western town in cahoots with a corrupt sheriff, the boxing commissions give the Promoter-Alphabet cartels a green light to manipulate the system. They have given a disordered sport some semblance of order—but at what price?

If weak boxing commissions won't act, it's up to the boxers themselves to join together and refuse to pay sanctioning fees. If they stick together, they will win because without fighters there is no sport. Let the sanctioning organizations give out all the titles they want, but without access to fees the days of these hustlers using pro boxing as their personal ATM would end. All that said, the chance of fighters staging a strike is slim. Most professional boxers live in the moment and dream of the next big payday. Staging a strike is a step many would be unwilling to take, especially if it might endanger their chance to achieve that big payday.

So what can be done? Even if all the elements of boxing's balkanized infrastructure remain intact, even if the sanctioning organizations and their promoter partners continue to stain the sport, even if the number of fabricated titles rises, much can still be done to make boxing safer for the people getting punched.

The first step in mitigating the danger—adopt the rule changes proposed in this book. Considering that most of today's prizefights are crude battles of attrition, we can decrease damage immediately by reducing the number of scheduled rounds, borrowing from MMA (see chapter three). And no matter how many rounds a fight is scheduled for, we must also improve the training and increase the accountability of both referees and ringside physicians.

If professional boxing is ever going to correct its flaws, it must uproot the corrupt interests that profit from the sport as it is currently organized. The goal isn't just to return to one undisputed champion for each weight division, but also to end an easily corrupted infrastructure and rating system that continue to endanger fighters.

AN ALTERNATIVE RATING SYSTEM

A reliable and honest ratings organization already exists that can and should replace the WBC, WBA, IBF, and WBO—the Transnational Boxing Rankings Board (TBRB), which operates much like the old National Boxing Association but has yet to get the same level of recognition. The TBRB is an all-volunteer initiative formed in October 2012 to provide pro boxing with authoritative top-ten rankings. The organization's website describes their mission as follows:

"To identify the singular world champion of every division by strict reasoning and common sense, and to insist on the sport's reform. Board membership includes fifty respected boxing journalists and record keepers from around the world who are uncompromised by so-called sanctioning bodies and promoters."

The reason the sport's power brokers ignore the TBRB is obvious—their ratings can't be bought or manipulated.

Eliminating the sanctioning organizations will take a miracle, but whether or not they remain, if even a few of the rules and safety protocols proposed in this book are incorporated into the sport, it would make a big difference—in saving boxers, not only from themselves but also from a corrupt, destructive environment.

• • •

If hope is on the horizon for boxing, it may come from the recent multibillion-dollar merger of the UFC (Ultimate Fighting Championship) and the WWE (World Wrestling Entertainment). It could be a game changer if this new entity—fittingly called TKO Group Holdings— decides to buy out every boxing promoter, clean house, and eliminate the sanctioning organizations. (See chapter eighteen.) Of course, even if this happens, there are no guarantees the situation will improve under their auspices. Meaningful improvement will come only from people who sincerely want to change the current dynamic and help the sport regain a semblance of integrity and trust.

CHAPTER 17

Analysis of Fourteen Title Bouts That Ended in a Fatality

From 1995 to 2022, 119 boxers died from punishment sustained during a professional prizefight.[122] Of that number thirteen were killed in a title fight and one in an "eliminator." All these fights were sanctioned by an Alphabet organization—eight by the WBC; five by the IBF; and one by the WBO. Twelve of the fights were scheduled for twelve rounds. The other two were ten rounders.

My aim in analyzing these fights is to find any patterns that offer clues about what went wrong so that the same mistakes aren't made in the future. The most repetitive and damaging pattern I've found was that these fights were scheduled for too many rounds. Consider this: Six of the title fights ended in the twelfth round, three in the eleventh round, and four in the tenth. The only fatal fight that ended before the tenth round (a sixth round KO) involved a washed up thirty-six-year-old with a losing record who hadn't fought in three years. In addition, eleven of the bouts involved a minor subsidiary title that had never existed before the 1990s. With hundreds of fabricated ten- and twelve-round Alphabet titles and eliminators contested every year, we can expect more fighters to be put at risk—ones who should be fighting eight rounds or fewer.

My accounts of the fourteen fights described in this chapter include a summary and an explanation of what could have been done to prevent unnecessary death.

Key to Symbols: The record for each fighter is shown next to his name: (Won-Lost-Draw). The round the fatal fight ended is shown just before the scheduled distance (e.g., WKO 8/12).

WKO—Won by knockout. Fighter is counted out.

WTKO—Won by technical knockout. The referee or doctor stops the contest.

WD and LD—In fights that went the scheduled distance, the winner was decided by a points score as determined by three judges (e.g., **WD 10/10** or **LD 10/10**).

1. May 6, 1995
Gabriel Ruelas (40-2) WTKO 11/12 Jimmy Garcia (35-4)
Location: Las Vegas
Division: Super Featherweight
Title: WBC Super Featherweight

Summary: Garcia won only one round on the scorecards. He was battered severely by Ruelas throughout the fight. During the tenth round both Roy Jones Jr. and Larry Merchant, doing ringside commentary for HBO, were telling the TV audience that the fight should be stopped. Before the eleventh round began, the Nevada boxing commission's ringside physician visited Garcia but—to the dismay of Jones and Merchant—allowed the bout to continue. The referee finally stopped the fight in the eleventh round, but it was too late. Garcia collapsed in his corner, and within thirty-five minutes was undergoing surgery to relieve a blood clot on his brain. He never regained consciousness and died thirteen days later.

Cause: Abuse and negligence. Here we see yet another fight that featured a relatively unknown boxer who was moved into the WBC ratings to justify an easy defense for a popular champion. Ruelas was an experienced boxer-puncher who held victories over several legitimate contenders. Garcia's 35-4 record was misleading. Twenty-one of his thirty-nine opponents had never won a professional fight, and only seven had more wins than losses. Thirteen months earlier, Garcia had been knocked out by an opponent making his professional debut. Against Ruelas, Garcia was totally outclassed and appeared almost frail. It was obvious he didn't belong in the same ring with Ruelas— despite his phony WBC top-ten rating. There were also rumors (unverified) that the twenty-three-year-old fighter was weakened by his efforts to lose fifteen to thirty pounds in the two months before the fight to make the 130-pound weight limit. Whether the rumors were true or not, the referee and doctor waited much too long to stop a fight that should never have been allowed in the first place.

2. September 12, 1999
Kabary Salem (11-1) WTKO 10/12 Randie Carver (23-0)
Location: Kansas City
Division: Light Heavyweight
Title: North American Boxing Federation Light Heavyweight (WBC affiliate)

Summary: Newspaper accounts of the fight indicate that it wasn't handled properly by the referee. Carver head-butted repeatedly during the early rounds of a foul-filled bout. The referee did not respond to the repeated fouls, choosing to remain a passive spectator. Carver was knocked down in the tenth round and tried unsuccessfully four times to get to his feet. After he lost consciousness, paramedics worked on him for about twenty minutes in the ring. He was then taken to a hospital, where he died two days after emergency brain surgery.

Cause: Undetermined. The headbutts were probably a contributing factor, but without video of the fight it is difficult to know what went wrong. The referee appears to have lost control of the fight and would have been justified in disqualifying Salem for the repeated headbutts.

3. November 20, 1999
Paul Vaden (28-2) WKO 10/12 Stephan Johnson (27-8-1)
Location: Atlantic City
Division: Middleweight
Title: IBF Super Welterweight

Summary: Johnson was slightly ahead on the scorecards when Vaden landed two punches in the tenth round that knocked him down. When he failed to regain consciousness, Johnson was rushed to Atlantic City Medical Center, where he underwent emergency brain surgery. He died two weeks later.

Cause: Abuse and negligence. This tragedy could have been avoided had state boxing commissions lived up to their stated purpose of protecting the fighter. Johnson was under medical suspension by the Ontario Athletic Commission because of an eleventh-round knockout he had suffered seven months earlier for something called the World Boxing Federation World Super Welterweight title. Johnson was knocked unconscious in that fight and carried from the ring on a stretcher and briefly hospitalized. He subsequently underwent a CT scan that would have cleared him to fight again, but since he didn't complete the rest of the neurological examination, Canadian authorities refused to lift the suspension. It should also be noted that Johnson wore an artificial lens in one eye. He got past negligent state boxing commissions by leaving medical forms blank. Four months after being hospitalized Johnson was granted a license to fight in South Carolina, where he won a ten-round decision. Two months after that, in Albany, Georgia, he knocked out someone with a 9-60 record. After another six weeks, Johnson was cleared by New Jersey boxing officials to fight Vaden.

4. June 15, 2001
Andres Fernandez (16-5-1) WD 12/12 Jorge Alberto Reyes (21-16-2)
Location: Ancona, New Mexico
Division: Super Bantamweight
Title: North American Boxing Association Super Bantamweight (affiliate of the WBC)

Summary: After he won a unanimous decision, Fernandez said he wasn't feeling well and then lapsed into a coma. Rushed to a hospital, he underwent emergency brain surgery for a subdural hematoma. He remained hospitalized and regained consciousness but suffered from profound brain damage and never fully recovered. He eventually succumbed to his injuries, on December 16, 2005.

Cause: Undetermined. A minor title fight between two mediocre talents with unimpressive records should not have been scheduled for twelve rounds. Even so, the bout didn't ring any alarm bells beforehand. There is no video of the fight. This was one of the rare occasions where the winner of the bout suffered the fatal injury. Without more information, it is impossible to make any assumptions—other than that, in a dangerous contact sport, deaths can happen. Despite the lack of definitive information, we can say with certainty that this was yet another fight that should never have been scheduled for twelve rounds.

5. February 28, 2004
Ricky Quiles (34-6-3) WD 12/12 Luis Villalta (30-6-1)
Location: Coconut Creek, Florida
Division: Lightweight
Title: North American Boxing Association (NABA) Lightweight title (WBC affiliate)

Summary: Villalta collapsed moments after losing a unanimous decision. He died five days after undergoing surgery for head trauma.

Cause: Undetermined. At first glance, the fighters appeared to be evenly matched, but the thirty-five-year-old Villalta's record was deceiving. Twenty-two of his twenty-five KO victims were either debuting professionals or had had less than five fights, and he'd never beaten a name opponent. Quiles was a lighter puncher but had fought better opponents. Since the bout was for a minor regional title, it was scheduled for twelve rounds.

6. December 3, 2004
Ricardo Cordoba (22-0) WTKO 12/12 Carlos Meza (20-1-1)
Location: Colon, Panama
Division: Bantamweight
Title: WBC Latino Bantamweight

Summary: On paper this looked like an even match, since both boxers had the same number of fights. But eleven of Meza's twenty-two opponents had never won a fight, and eighteen of them never made it past the fourth round. This was Meza's first fight outside of his home country of Colombia, and he had only one previous ten-round bout—a points loss—whereas Cordoba had fought better competition and gone ten or more rounds five times. Shortly after the fight was stopped, Meza fell into a coma. He underwent emergency brain surgery that same night for a subdural hematoma. He never regained consciousness and died on December 7.

Cause: Abuse. Without video of the fight, it cannot be determined if the fight should have been stopped sooner. However, if you consider Meza's limited experience, the fight should have been scheduled for six or eight rounds. This was another fight stretched to twelve rounds to justify collecting a sanctioning fee for a phony title.

7. September 17, 2005
Jesus Chavez (41-3) WTKO 11/12 Leavander Johnson (34-4-2)
Location: Las Vegas
Division: Lightweight
Title: IBF World Lightweight

Summary: Thirty-five-year-old Leavander Johnson had fought only three bouts in the previous two years. According to BoxRec.com, "Johnson was never in the fight and was dominated, taking a pounding in the later rounds." Chavez was way ahead in the scoring. Johnson was hit hard in the head during both the tenth and eleventh rounds, but he was still standing when the referee finally stopped the uneven contest. While walking back to the dressing room, Johnson began dragging his leg. He was taken by ambulance to a hospital, where surgery for a subdural hematoma was performed within the hour. He died five days later.

Cause: Negligence. The referee and ringside physicians waited too long to stop this mismatch. Johnson had taken continuous punishment throughout the fight. It would have ended before the tenth round if a rule were in place that automatically stops a bout if one of the boxers has lost three one-sided rounds by a score of 10-8 or 10-7 on all three judges' scorecards. But even with such a rule in force, judges would have had to be instructed not to automatically award nine points to the loser of a round without considering how much punishment he has taken.

8. December 25, 2007
Yo-Sam Choi (31-5) WD 12/12 Heri Amol (22-7)
Location: Seoul, South Korea
Division: Flyweight
Title: WBO Intercontinental Flyweight

Summary: This is another rare instance of a victorious fighter who collapsed after winning a decision. Thirty-four-year-old Choi had been a pro for fourteen years and was a former light-flyweight champion (WBC 1993–2002). Against Amol, he was defending a recently won WBO Inter-Continental Flyweight title for the first time. Choi was way ahead on points when he was knocked down with five seconds remaining in the twelfth round. He beat the count and went on to win a unanimous decision. Moments after the decision was announced, Choi collapsed and was rushed to a hospital, where he underwent emergency brain surgery. He died eight days later without regaining consciousness.

Cause: Undetermined. It's difficult to know if Choi's age was a factor, but allowing a thirty-four-year-old boxer to fight a twelve-rounder for some obscure title was not in his best interest.

9. October 15, 2008
Alejandro Sanabria (16-0) WKO 12/12 Daniel Aguillon (14-3-2)
Location: Polanco, Mexico
Division: Super Featherweight
Title: WBC FECARBOX Super Featherweight (FECARBOX is an acronym for the Federacion Centroamericana de Boxeo Profesional—the Central American arm of the WBC)

Summary: Aguillon was knocked down in the first round but came back to drop Sanabria in the fourth. In a hard-fought, close bout, Sanabria was slightly ahead in the scoring going into the final round. In the last minute of the twelfth round, Aguillon was knocked out by a right to the jaw. The unconscious fighter was taken to a hospital but remained in a coma and died five days later.

Cause: Abuse. What should have been an ordinary eight-round preliminary contest between two inexperienced boxers was upgraded to the twelve-round championship distance for no other reason than to generate a sanctioning fee for another synthetic WBC title. Only five of Aguillon's previous nineteen fights had gone beyond six rounds. Before this bout he'd lost an eight-round decision to a fighter with a 6-6-1 record. A month before that, he won a four-round preliminary match against an opponent who hadn't won a fight. In terms of his experience and physical condition, Aguillon was not ready to engage in a tough twelve-round contest.

10. November 20, 2009
Teon Kennedy (13-0-1) WTKO 10/12 Francisco Rodriguez (14-2)
Location: Philadelphia, Pennsylvania
Division: Super Bantamweight
Title: IBF USBA Super Bantamweight

Summary: Rodriguez (14-2) was staggered and nearly knocked out by Kennedy (13-0) in the first round, but he recovered sufficiently to give Kennedy all he could handle over the next seven rounds. The action was fast and furious. At the end of the eighth round, Kennedy had a slight lead in the scoring. The ninth round turned deadly for Rodriguez and marked the turning point in the bout. Kennedy took charge, landing several damaging punches. The ringside physician checked on Rodriguez several times in between rounds to monitor his condition and said he saw no evidence that the fighter was in distress. Kennedy continued his attack in the tenth round. At 1:52 the referee ended the contest to save Rodriguez from further punishment. Moments later Rodriguez slumped to the floor, unconscious. Despite emergency brain surgery to relieve pressure on his brain caused by a subdural hematoma, Rodriguez never regained consciousness and died forty-eight hours later.

Cause: Negligence. This was an exciting and competitive contest between fighters with similar records, but it should have been scheduled for six or eight rounds at most. Neither fighter had the experience needed to engage in a punishing ten- or twelve-round bout at this stage of his career. Without film of the fight, we don't know if the referee or doctor should have stopped it earlier, but the doctor's entrance into the ring "on several occasions" to check on Rodriguez shows he had genuine concern about the fighter's condition. Nevertheless, he appeared reluctant to stop the fight.

11. November 5, 2018
Don Parueang (6-4) WKO 12/12 Christian Daghio (11-0)
Location: Rangsit, Thailand

Division: Light Heavyweight
Title: Vacant WBC Asian Boxing Council Silver Light Heavyweight

Summary: Forty-nine-year-old Christian Daghio faced thirty-seven-year-old Don Parueang for another absurd twelve-round WBC fake title bout. The YouTube video of the fight shows two out-of-condition, middle-aged fighters with primitive boxing skills. The first five rounds were tame and uneventful, although Daghio was taking more head punishment than his opponent. By the seventh round, both fighters were near exhaustion. Yet Daghio kept moving forward, which only increased the concussive effect of the hundred or more punches that struck his head. Shortly after the twelfth round started, Daghio was dropped by a right to the chin. He beat the count but was still groggy when he was hit by two more punches. Daghio was unconscious before his head slammed against the ring floor. He died a week later.

Cause: Abuse. Before switching to boxing in 2015, at age forty-six, Daghio had competed successfully for many years in the combat sport of Muay Thai. He also had fought one MMA bout, losing by decision. As revealed in the YouTube video, his boxing skills—and his opponent's—were on the amateur level. Age alone should have disqualified Daghio from competing, let alone fighting a twelve-round match. The fact that either of these boxers competed for a professional championship is appalling. But the WBC needs its sanctioning fees.

12. July 19, 2019
Subriel Matias (13-0) WTKO 11/12 Maxim Dadashev (13-0)
Location: Oxon Hill, Maryland
Division: Super Lightweight
Title: IBF Super Lightweight Title Eliminator

Summary: Even though this fight was not technically for an Alphabet title, the IBF Eliminator label mandated a twelve-round bout, which ignored the fact that both fighters were woefully inexperienced. The fight was competitive up to the seventh round. From then on Dadashev began to wilt under Matias's constant pressure. Matias landed many damaging punches to Dadashev's head over the next three rounds. Between the eleventh and twelfth round, Dadashev's trainer, Buddy McGirt, signaled to the referee that his fighter had had enough, and the fight was stopped. Dadashev collapsed after he exited the ring. He was hospitalized in critical condition and underwent emergency brain surgery for a subdural hematoma. Dadashev died four days later.

Cause: As explained in chapter two, both negligence and incompetence played a role here. Dadashev had only sixty-seven rounds of professional boxing experience. Despite a deep amateur background, he wasn't ready for a twelve-round fight against a tough opponent that early in his career. When an Alphabet organization can't come up with another title name to justify a sanctioning fee, they conveniently call the fight a title eliminator, which requires twelve rounds and a fee. A match of six or eight rounds would have been safer.

13. October 12, 2019
Charles Conwell (10-0) WTKO 10/10 Patrick Day (17-3-1)
Location: Chicago, Illinois
Division: Super Welterweight
Title: IBF USBA Super Welterweight

Summary: Day was knocked down in the fourth round and again in the eighth by right-hand punches to his head. He was behind on the scorecards, having won only two of the previous seven rounds. The bell rang to end the eighth round before action could resume following the knockdown. Day appeared unsteady on his legs as he returned to his corner. He made it through the ninth round, but eighty seconds into the tenth, Day was hit with another right, which staggered him. Immediately after that, he was hit by two quick follow-up punches that knocked him backward and down. The back of Day's head slammed hard against the ring floor. The unconscious boxer underwent emergency brain surgery for a subdural hematoma. He never regained consciousness and died four days later.

Cause: The details of this fight can also be found in chapter two. It's difficult to say who was at fault. The fight was hard-fought and brutal through the eighth round. The video doesn't include the crucial ninth round. But under the rules proposed in this book it would have been scheduled for no more than five rounds.

14. October 16, 2021
David Contreras (19-0) KO 6/10 Moises Fuentes (25-6-1)
Location: Cancun, Mexico
Division: Flyweight
Title: WBC Youth Silver Super Flyweight

Summary: As detailed in chapter two, champion Moises Fuentes was launching an ill-advised comeback at age thirty-six after having retired three years earlier. Before he retired, he had lost four of his last five fights, including two by knockout. His timing and reflexes were way off, and he was an open target for his opponent's punches. Contreras dominated the fight, winning the first five rounds. In the sixth round, a left hook to the jaw dropped Fuentes hard. The back of his head slammed against the ring floor. The unconscious boxer was hospitalized, and brain surgery was performed. Fuentes never regained consciousness and succumbed to his injuries a month later.

Cause: Negligence. It was irresponsible for the WBC to allow a thirty-six-year-old boxer who was coming off a three-year layoff—and had lost his previous two fights by knockout—to engage in a title fight against an undefeated, hard-punching prospect.

CHAPTER 18

The Future of Professional Boxing: An Interview with Promoter Lou DiBella

From 1989 to 2000, Lou DiBella worked at HBO, becoming Senior Vice President of HBO Sports. During his tenure, HBO became the preeminent boxing network. The Harvard Law School graduate was also the creative force behind HBO's highly successful *Boxing after Dark* series.

In 2000, DiBella left his position at HBO and started DiBella Entertainment, a boxing promotional company, where he created the popular monthly televised series *Broadway Boxing*. Some of the boxing stars he has promoted include Bernard Hopkins, Sergio Martinez, Jermain Taylor, Ike Quartey, Paulie Malignaggi, Andre Berto, Yuri Foreman, Micky Ward, Dmitry Salita, and many others. Lou has also promoted female boxing champions such as Amanda Serrano and Heather Hardy. Over the years, DiBella Entertainment has expanded into book publishing as well as TV and feature film production. A lifelong lover of baseball, Lou also owns two AA Minor League Baseball teams.

Lou DiBella isn't your typical boxing promoter. According to his company's website: "DBE rejects the contractual exploitation of professional boxers and employs a business model that at once shifts the balance of power from promoters to boxers, and establishes a legacy of matchmaking excellence to elevate the sport of boxing."

To survive in the dog-eat-dog world of professional boxing, DiBella has to be a tough and savvy businessman, but unlike the Bob Arums and Don Kings of boxing, he genuinely loves the sport, respects its fans, and always conducts his business with boxing's best interests in mind. In fact, the Boxing Writers Association of America honored Lou with their James A. Farley Award for Honesty and Integrity in Boxing in 2016. If professional boxing were ever to get a federal boxing commissioner, Lou DiBella would be the ideal choice for the position.[123]

THE INTERVIEW

MS: Lou, despite all its troubles and critics, professional boxing, although not the mainstream sport it once was, still maintains a strong international presence and is not likely to be counted out anytime soon.

LD: People will always fight for other people's entertainment; people will always fuck for other people's entertainment. There will always be people fighting each other and getting paid for it, and there will always be pornography because sex and fighting are in our DNA. So boxing is not going away. It's not disappearing. No matter how low we go, it will continue to exist and continue to metamorphose into something.

MS: Are you optimistic about boxing's future?

LD: No, not if it maintains the status quo. The paradigm that exists in professional boxing from a business, administrative, ratings, and championship perspective doesn't work. At present, there is a completely unhealthy administration for the sport. Yes, we are still capable of having huge [paydays]; yes, people's interest in fighting is so incredible that now film celebrities, YouTube influencers, prostitutes, strippers, ex-athletes, even senior citizens—anyone—can put on boxing gloves and get paid to fight if they have enough of a social media presence or enough celebrity recognition.

MS: Whose fault is that?

LD: We have done such a poor job overall of being custodians of the sweet science. There are four major [sanctioning] organizations, not counting the ones that aren't major—which, by the way, aren't necessarily worse than the major ones. There are at least six too many weight classes, all of which now seem to have not only the "regular" champions but also "interim" or even "super" champions all reigning at the same time. So, basically, you could have eight or more fighters calling themselves world champions in the same weight class.

MS: What about the argument that having multiple champions in the same weight class gives unknown fighters a chance to gain some recognition and prestige?

LD: Ninety-nine percent of fighters are earning money below the poverty line worldwide. There are fighters who continue to fight into their forties and fifties because they never had health benefits, couldn't save any money, and are destined to not know how to do anything except fight. There are Mountain Riveras all over boxing. (Note: DiBella is referring to the fictional and pathetic, broken-down ex-fighter portrayed in the classic film *Requiem for a Heavyweight*.)

MS: Let me put the question another way: Do the sanctioning organizations serve any useful purpose?

LD: Well, right now there's nobody else giving out belts or ratings. Yes, they serve a useful purpose, but there are three too many of them—there should be one. The reality is the whole system, and that includes sanctioning fees and picking judges, is corrupt. Out of the four major ratings organizations, only one of them addresses the use of performance-enhancing drugs. The truth is the whole sport is basically byzantine at this point.

MS: My book's focus is how to make professional boxing safer despite the byzantine nature of the business. One of the problems, as I see it, is the poor performance of many referees.

LD: There is no system of checks and balances for bad officials. The ratings organizations are to blame, as well as the state boxing commissions. All the boxing commissions, both here and overseas, are politicized bodies that are protecting nobody. They know nothing about the sport for the most part, and their oversight and administration couldn't be much worse.

MS: You have been one of boxing's major promoters for over thirty years.

LD: And, for a full decade, I've been trying to figure out a way to extricate myself from this. So arguably, yes, I've made a good living out of it; yes, I'm one of the decision makers; and yes, I've gotten myself into the International Boxing Hall of Fame. But I think, right now, where we are is a place that suggests to me the sport needs an entire reboot.

MS: If you could, how would you "reboot" it?

LD: It's not how I would do it, because no one can do it. It's Dodge City, and there's no superhero marshal who's going to clean up boxing right now. What probably would have to happen is similar to what happened to Mixed Martial Arts [MMA]. In the 1990s, they went into the toilet bowl, and somebody invested a crazy amount of money in them and then changed the rules, and now the UFC [Ultimate Fighting Championship] is the largest MMA organization in the world and has a de facto monopoly position in MMA.

MS: Are you suggesting professional boxing should model itself after the UFC?

LD: In April [2023], the UFC announced a merger with the WWE [World Wrestling Entertainment], the largest professional wrestling promotion company in the world. If the UFC people—now that they're partnered with the WWE—came into boxing and said, "Fuck it, I'm ignoring all the ratings organizations. I'm going to set up my own rankings, my own belts, and I'm going to put fighters under contract and give them healthcare. I'm also going to drive down the numbers so that the richest fighters are going to make way, way less money, but the average fighter is going to make way more money." In that scenario, I think they'd have great success.

MS: But realistically, do you ever see that happening?

LD: Yes, I do see that happening because I see the sport tanking. Right now, Al Haymon, Robert Arum, Eddie Hearn, Oscar De La Hoya, and Frank Warren haven't invested much into the business. Don't you think the people that run the WWE and the people that run the UFC so successfully could create a similar business model and make a venture into boxing? They certainly are better performers in terms of television product than any of the television product boxing's putting out there. But what that is going to do is put a lot of people in traditional boxing out of work, because I don't think they [UFC and WWE are] going to do business with the sanctioning organizations. Certainly not with four of them.

MS: So you think the UFC might be interested in making a move into the professional boxing business?

LD: It's not the UFC! As I said, the UFC has merged with the WWE. They are now a newly formed twenty-billion-dollar, publicly traded combat sports company known as TKO Group Holdings. A billion dollars would buy every boxing business of significance around the world. And, by the way, no one would find the need to purchase them because if someone came in with the appropriate money, you don't need to buy anyone.

MS: Please clarify.

LD: The few superstars in boxing are getting older right now and are expungable pretty much. The UFC and WWE, with their track record of success, could easily go out and get a television contract. That's what you need— a television contract. And then you need someone with the balls to try to change the rules of the game, because, right now, boxing, as it's presently set up, has failed.

MS: The Terence Crawford vs. Errol Spence title fight reportedly had over 650,000 domestic pay-per-view buys at eighty-four dollars per buy. That's a nice gross of over fifty-four million dollars.

LD: Who cares? It's one night. Big deal. Even if they did sell 650,000 buys, so what? It's two nights a year. The NFL [National Football League] does it seventeen times a week during football season.

MS: Are you saying that if a huge corporate entity came in with a billion dollars, got rid of the sanctioning organizations, and restructured the sport, the business would change for the better?

LD: Although I think someone's going to come in and rewrite the industry, it doesn't necessarily mean it's all going to be good. Right now, boxing is a niche sport, and we've had a good year so far. Most people who follow boxing would say 2023 is an up year. But it's a good year for a niche sport; it's not a good year for boxing when it was the sport of kings—when boxing was a major sport. It's a good year for boxing in the niche it has been in for the last twenty years, and particularly in the last five years, since the demise of HBO Sports. Right now, things are so fractured and so open to change that there is going to be a change in the paradigm of boxing sometime in the next decade.

MS: And perhaps bring new leadership to the sport?

LD: You are going to see boxing look very different than it looks right now. I'm telling you, someone with money is going to come in and rewrite the rules. It's inevitable. A huge corporate entity is going to redefine boxing. That's my prediction. You may not love it if you're a purist, or maybe you will like it. To be honest, as far as I'm concerned, it can't be much worse than it is right now.

MS: What worries me is that you said it may not change for the better. I'm not optimistic, considering boxing's history.

LD: In certain ways it may not change significantly for the better because there are other aspects to consider. Go to BoxRec.com [an internet site containing the win-loss record of every professional boxer], and you will see all of these MMA guys who have never had a pro boxing match, or have had one fight against a Jake Paul [an American social media personality and neophyte boxer with a huge YouTube and Instagram following and also co-founder of a boxing promotion company], or whatever, and they are listed on BoxRec. Jake Paul has a worldwide ranking on BoxRec. So what I am saying is that we are already metamorphosing. It may not necessarily be for the better, but I tell you this: from a business standpoint, it will be more rational. I don't know if it's going to be for the better if you are a purist and a fan of the sport. But I do know it will have a better business paradigm in a decade. It doesn't necessarily mean you will like what you are watching if you are an old-school historian.

MS: Well, I consider myself a purist and an old-school boxing historian, but I'll certainly be glad when we do away with the old system.

LD: No, it's not going to do away with the old system—it's going to kill it. Someone is going to come in and get a TV deal and build it up the way they built up the UFC. There are still MMA promotions all over the world, but they're just worth shit compared to the UFC. That's what's going to happen to boxing. There is going to be one preeminent organization worldwide, and it's going to be done as a business and change the rules of the game. As I said earlier, maybe not all for what you view as for the better. If you're a purist, certainly not. But it's going to make it a more economically reasonable paradigm. It's also probably going to provide more opportunity for the working-class fighter because, right now, all the money is being made by a handful of fighters. All across the world, boxers are fighting for basically poverty-level pay.

MS: I look forward to writing about and encouraging the change you're predicting.

LD: You don't need to encourage anything. As I said, it is inevitable. Look at the world of combat sports today from a historian's perspective. Look at the merger between the UFC and WWE. They are a publicly traded company capitalized to twenty billion dollars. Notice they call themselves TKO Group Holdings. It will trade on the New York Stock

Exchange under the ticker TKO. What kind of term is "TKO"? Isn't that a boxing term?

MS: You said boxing was having a good year in 2023. Doesn't that mean a major promoter like Bob Arum also had a good year?

LD: Do you think ESPN really needs Bob Arum to survive? ESPN is hurting desperately. You know who ESPN right now cares about more than anyone? The UFC and WWE. Professional wrestling is a bigger worldwide media property than all of boxing put together across the world. The WWE alone is a huge entity. You don't think they're in a good position to get a television deal if they launch a boxing branch? They are in the best position. It is almost self-apparent. Somebody is going to do this. And that somebody is also going to figure out that the concept of doing exclusive deals with one promoter has fractured the sport of boxing hopelessly and has been one of the real impediments to change. It stops the biggest and best fights from happening. Not only will there be no more multiple sanctioning bodies, there will be no more promoters. King and Arum, the guys that are going to be in this until they drop dead, are a thing of the past. There are no promoters, plural, in MMA anymore. There is one promoter—it's the UFC.

MS: Having only one promoter would certainly be preferable to having a bunch of rival promoters and sanctioning organizations creating confusion and chaos by each recognizing their own world champions and title contenders.

LD: That's probably where it's heading, and the only way it's going to get fixed. Boxing needs a central administration and central governance and somebody with an incentive to run a rational business that's not corrupt. Why are football, baseball, and hockey not more corrupt than they already are? It's because they are gigantic and have huge followings. If people were watching NFL games and the results were rigged constantly, the NFL would lose their TV deals. They would lose everything. Right now, you don't hear as many controversies over scoring or judging in MMA as you do in boxing.

MS: While waiting for the changes you predict, we still have to consider how to make boxing a safer sport. I am distressed at the poor performance of boxing officials, specifically referees and ringside physicians, who are tasked with protecting the fighters.

LD: The terrible officiating we often see is built into the existing structure. For example: how are sanctioning fees determined? The sanctioning organization takes a percentage of the fighters' purses. So the sanctioning body wants the A-side [i.e., more popular and salable] fighter to win. And they appoint judges and referees who are associated with their organization and who know what the organization wants. You know, people use the term "institutional racism"; professional boxing has institutionalized corruption.

MS: How can athletic commissions, specifically throughout the United States, help to improve fighter safety?

LD: There needs to be standardized health and safety regulations. A lot of states don't even require MRIs, and a lot of states license a fighter who's been knocked out seventeen times in a row.

MS: But even in a state with an adequate medical testing protocol that includes MRIs and prohibits obvious mismatches, the competence of the referee makes a huge difference.

LD: Right now, there are referees who should not be working a fight because they don't know shit. Rabbit punches [a blow to the back of the head or the base of the skull] are the most deadly thing in boxing, and you see them in every single fight, yet the referees often don't even warn the fighters against using them.

MS: You often see the same incompetent referees getting assignments every week.

LD: Well, they are getting the assignments because they are politically appointed by the ratings organizations. They are getting assigned to bigger fights because of their association with them. Bad referees continue to work because they are advancing the agenda of the ratings organization. It's not like Mauricio Sulaiman [president of the WBC] is saying to them, "Hey, Canelo's got to win." The referees and judges go to the sanctioning body conventions. They're around everybody. They understand the system. Do you think it's any accident that there is at least one outrageous scorecard for the A-side fighter in almost every meaningful fight?

MS: It would be a great improvement if the ratings organizations had no influence in choosing referees or judges. The referee should be selected at random. Why not have the names of six or seven qualified referees placed in a drum at the state athletic commission offices and chosen by lottery?

LD: It wouldn't make a difference, not if the state athletic commission is going to be no better than the ratings organization. There has to be oversight by somebody, but the reality is it's part of why the whole paradigm is broken. In the United States, there are half a dozen athletic commissions worth a shit. That's in the United States. What do you think it is like in the rest of the world? Most of the referees suck, and most of the officials suck.

MS: I would add there is also very little oversight when it comes to the performance of the ringside physicians.

LD: Well, they should be neurologists or certainly have some kind of expertise with neurological symptoms and concussions. But the problem goes beyond fixing; it goes beyond suggestions. Nothing's going to help unless you tear the whole fucking system down. How are you going to change anything within the broken system that exists? In many states, all you need to fight is an AIDS test and an eye test. The states are as bad, or worse, than the ratings organizations.

MS: But the effort has to be made to at least try to change things.

LD: You want to know the truth, Mike? You love the sport too much, and you don't want to say what you already know. If they are not going to fix the shit, then it should be banned. It's killing people. It's brain damaging people. And most of them are not even making a living. The sport is set up in a way that you're not protecting anybody. So if you want the real bottom line, if you are coming at this from a health and safety standpoint, do away with it.

MS: But the reality is that boxing will not be abolished, and with that in mind, I hope your prediction of a new entity changing the paradigm— hopefully for the better—will come true.

In Lou DiBella's interview, he accurately predicted that "A huge corporate entity is going to redefine boxing."

The plan is for the TKO group to create a boxing league that strives to change the way the sport operates. The new league will use a tournament format similar to that of the UFC. It remains to be seen, but if done right this could turn out to be the game changer that boxing desperately needs.

• • •

As this book was about to be typeset, it was announced that TKO Group Holdings had formed a multiyear partnership with the Saudi General Entertainment Authority, to launch a new boxing promotion starting in 2026. Dana White, CEO and President of the Ultimate Fighting Championship (UFC), will manage the day-to-day operations of the new boxing venture, which is part of Saudi Arabia's extensive investment in global sports. The first co-promotion between White and the Saudi General Entertainment Authority is the Canelo Alvarez vs. Terence Crawford undisputed super middleweight world championship on September 13, 2025, in Las Vegas.

CHAPTER 19

Summary of Recommended Changes to Laws and Regulations

I. GENERAL

a. Reduce the Maximum Number of Scheduled Rounds. Every prizefight involves calculated risk for its participants. But as a fight progresses from one round to the next the risk only grows, especially if boxing's safety nets—the referee and ringside physicians—fail to act in time (see chapter four). To mitigate the incidence of head trauma and give the boxer a safer work environment, the number of scheduled rounds needs to be adjusted. This would offset the presence of feckless boxing commissions and incompetent or compromised referees and ringside physicians. (See chapters four and nine.) Statistics show that a five-round distance is safest (see chapter two). That said, if we want to make the sport as safe as possible—without turning it into amateur boxing—most pro bouts should be scheduled for five rounds (or four for preliminary bouts). Fights scheduled for six, eight, or ten rounds can be permitted, but only under certain circumstances that match boxers with similar skills and experience. Twelve-round bouts should be outlawed by every state and country because the glut of fabricated twelve-round Alphabet titles and eliminators have endangered the lives and health of fighters who can't handle the distance (see chapters sixteen and seventeen).

As an added safety precaution, no boxer should be allowed to engage in a bout that exceeds six rounds until he has accumulated a minimum of fifty professional rounds.

b. Standing Eight Count. (See chapter six.) If a fighter momentarily slumps after taking a punch—indicating a brief loss of consciousness (a mini-concussion)—is staggered, or if he is hit by a series of punches and appears unable to retaliate or escape, the referee will stop the action, order the boxer's opponent to a neutral corner, and start an eight count. The point of the standing eight count is to interrupt the attack when the opponent is particularly vulnerable to injury. An alert fighter can see a punch coming toward him, and if he can't avoid it, he'll reflexively tense his neck muscles to lessen the shock of the punch. If the fighter is not alert, the unseen punch will cause his head to whip around, which may result in a mini-concussion. If the fighter cannot avoid follow-up punches, the referee must stop the action and administer a standing eight count. This will give the referee sufficient time to evaluate the fighter's condition and determine whether he can continue. A standing eight count may also be given at any time—even in the absence of a mini-concussion—when the referee determines that a fighter's defense is inadequate and he has taken too many punches. If the referee gives a third standing eight count to the same fighter in the same round, he'll declare the fight over and give a TKO (technical knockout) victory to the opponent.

c. Expand the Ringside Physician's Role. (See chapter nine.) A qualified ringside physician will be allowed to stop a fight during a round or between rounds without notifying the referee. To add an extra layer of safety, at every professional bout *two* qualified ringside physicians should be seated at opposite sides of the ring and have an unobstructed view of the fighters. Both doctors will have access to a timekeeper's bell or air horn. If either doctor decides a fighter has taken enough punishment, he will signal the referee to stop the fight with the bell or air horn. (He won't need to confer with the other doctor before making this decision.) On hearing the signal—air horn or bell—the referee must stop the fight immediately. He doesn't need to confer with the doctor because the doctor's decision to stop the fight is final.

Also, at the end of any round, the doctor may—at his discretion or if summoned by the referee—examine one or both fighters. The doctor will enter the ring, order the seconds out of his way, and face the fighter directly while taking ten to fifteen seconds—or more if necessary—questioning the fighter to determine his condition and decide whether to stop the bout. If the fight is allowed to continue, any time lost during this brief examination will be added to the rest period to give the fighter's seconds a full minute to minister to him.

d. Throwing in the Towel. (See chapter six.) Throwing a towel into the ring is considered an antiquated way to signal surrender and end a prizefight. Some jurisdictions allow it, while others don't. Those that don't allow it include Nevada and New York. In both states either an inspector (New York) or ringside doctor (Nevada) must first be notified by the fighter's chief second (usually the fighter's trainer) that he wants the fight stopped, after which the inspector or doctor signals the referee to stop the fight. But precious seconds are wasted in this two-step process, during which time the fighter will sustain further punishment. In California and Europe, the fight is immediately stopped if the chief second tosses a towel into the ring. This rule should be adopted in all boxing jurisdictions because the chief second—usually the fighter's trainer—often recognizes that his fighter risks serious harm before the referee or doctor does.

e. Referees and Ringside Physicians. Both referees and doctors must be made aware of studies showing that a third of ring fatalities have occurred in the last scheduled round of a fight (see chapter two). The referee should never allow his decision to stop a fight depend on how much time is left in the last scheduled round.

f. Rules Pertaining to the Mouthpiece. (See chapter six.) A fighter who deliberately spits out his mouthpiece twice during a fight will be automatically disqualified. After the first instance, the referee will warn the fighter that he will lose by disqualification if he spits out his mouthpiece a second time. A fighter will also be disqualified if he deliberately spits out the mouthpiece after being knocked down.

g. Return to Same-Day Weigh-Ins. The weigh-in will take place before noon on the day of the fight, as was the custom for many decades. (See chapter six.) This will encourage boxers to fight at their natural weight and avoid the excessive dehydration involved if they had to make weight the previous day. It would also help them avoid having to excessively rehydrate in the twenty-four hours after an early weigh-in.

h. Taping the Hands. (See chapter fifteen.) The taping of a fighter's hands must be monitored closely, so that the correct amount of tape and gauze are used, and no tampering takes place with either bandages or gloves. Too many commissions rely on an untrained "inspector" to be present in the dressing room when the bandages and tape are applied. The process will now take place in the ring before the bout. A commissioner and a representative from each fighter's corner will observe, feel, and approve both bandages and gloves.

II. SCORING

a. Only One Extra Point for a Knockdown. (See chapter eleven.) A knockdown will no longer automatically win the round for the fighter scoring the knockdown. The fighter may be rewarded an extra point for the knockdown, but his opponent can still win the round if he's connected with more punches in that round. The new rule will not only reward clever boxing, but it will prevent a round from being won unfairly simply because a boxer scored a knockdown while his opponent clearly dominated the rest of the round.

b. Point Score to Accurately Reflect the Action. Most boxing commissions use the "ten-point must system" for scoring fights. (See chapter eleven.) Ten points are awarded to the winner of a round and nine points or fewer to the loser. Too many judges automatically score a round 10-9 even if the winner of the round has dominated his opponent for three minutes and landed many more punches. Scoring must be more nuanced to accurately reflect what has happened in the round. This should not be difficult, as most boxing people can easily differentiate between a 10-7 or 10-8 round and a 10-9 round. Only close rounds will get a 10-9 score. Judges should also be more encouraged to score a round even (10-10) if they deem it too close to call for either fighter.

c. Rules for the Loss of Consecutive Rounds. If a fighter loses four consecutive rounds on all three judges' scorecards in a fight scheduled for five or more rounds, the referee and ringside physicians will be notified, at which point they will confer briefly between rounds and decide if the contest should continue or end in a TKO victory for the fighter scoring the shutout. In making the decision, the officials will need to consider context. If the boxer losing the rounds displays an adequate defense and hasn't taken much punishment, and the rounds have been close, the referee can decide to let the fight continue. If a fighter loses three rounds by a margin of two or more points on two judges' scorecards, the referee and ringside physicians must end the fight to prevent more damage from the mismatch. (See chapter eleven.)

III. EQUIPMENT

a. Head Guards Mandatory. (See chapter twelve.) A soccer-style head guard that covers the eyebrows to the hairline and is secured by a chin strap should be mandatory in all professional bouts. The soccer style guard is less obtrusive and bulky than the standard boxing head guard but can still prevent cuts around the orbital bone and lessen the impact of an accidental or intentional headbutt. The head guard must include a two- or three-inch-thick foam cushion that covers the back of the head. This prevents coup contrecoup concussions, which occur when the fighter falls backward and bangs the back of his head against the floor of the ring. The foam covering the back of the head should extend down to the base of the skull to prevent damage by an illegal—and potentially deadly—rabbit punch, a serious foul ignored by most referees and not even mentioned in many referees' pre-fight instructions.

b. Funding for Further Studies of Equipment. The state in which a multimillion-dollar pay-per-view fight takes place will tax the promoter, with proceeds going toward funding a scientific study of boxing gloves and head guards to determine which designs and materials can best diminish the concussive effect of a punch to the head.

IV. EDUCATION

Revamp Licensing Requirements for Referees, Ringside Physicians, and Trainers. (See chapters four, five and nine.) Attendance is required at approved courses and seminars that teach how to recognize the signs of concussion and the dangers of weight cutting. Taking these courses will be essential before licensing trainers, referees and ringside physicians. No current program effectively addresses these topics. As a licensing requirement, referees, ringside physicians, and trainers must pass a standardized test based on the aforementioned courses.

V. INFRASTRUCTURE

a. Reduce the Number of Weight Divisions. Only three to four pounds separate eight of the seventeen existing weight divisions. The weight differential will be expanded to seven pounds for the flyweight through welterweight divisions and nine pounds or more for divisions from middleweight through heavyweight. The number of weight divisions will not exceed twelve. The upper limits for the revised weight divisions are as follows:

Flyweight—112 pounds
Bantamweight –118 pounds
Featherweight—125 pounds
Lightweight—132 pounds
Light Welterweight—139 pounds
Welterweight—147 pounds
Light Middleweight—156 pounds
Middleweight—166 pounds
Light Heavyweight —177 pounds
Cruiserweight—200 pounds
Heavyweight—Over 200 pounds

b. Rules for Choosing the Referee and Judges. (See chapters seven and sixteen.) No promoter or sanctioning organization will be allowed to influence the selection of the referee or judges. This important decision will be made by the boxing commission of the country or state where the fight will take place. The names of the referees and judges will be randomly chosen from a pool of qualified candidates in the same way lottery winners are. The commission will not divulge the names of the referee or judges until immediately before the fight The referee will have more leeway to act in the fighters' best interest if he knows his next assignment won't be influenced by the whim or prejudice of a promoter or sanctioning organization.

In addition, no referee or judge will belong to any sanctioning organization or wear an organization's logo on their shirt while working a fight. Membership in a sanctioning organization will automatically disqualify a referee or judge from future assignments.

c. Payment to the Referee and Judges. Neither the promoter nor the sanctioning organization shall be responsible—directly or indirectly— for paying a referee's or judge's fee. To avoid conflicts of interest, the referee's and judges' fees should be set and paid by the boxing commission of the state or country where the bout is held.

d. Loss of Referee or Judge's License. Referees and judges will not have any social interaction or financial dealings with promoters or sanctioning organization representatives. A violation of this rule will result in the referee or judge losing their license. A referee or judge banned in one state cannot go to another jurisdiction to officiate. It will be up to the state or country's boxing commission to enforce this rule.

e. Abolish the WBC, WBA, IBF, and WBO. (See chapter 16.) No organization will be allowed to charge a fee to sanction a fight, a change that will effectively end the reign of the Alphabet organizations. Professional boxing must rid itself of these parasites if it's ever going to free itself from the corrupt and chaotic mess they've helped create, and in which they thrive.

CLOSING REFLECTIONS

Though boxing is by nature a dangerous sport, far too many fighters suffer unnecessary brain trauma and even lose their lives because of the ongoing corruption, incompetence, and abuse described in this book. That professional boxing still adheres to outdated rules only compounds the problem. Many tragedies could be prevented if basic protocols—or even simple common sense—is observed before or during fights.

I don't pretend to have all the answers to the myriad problems that pro boxing faces, nor do I expect everyone to agree with everything I've recommended. What is inarguable is this: every boxer who steps into the ring deserves the safest possible work environment while they pursue their dreams in an unforgiving sport.

Acknowledgments

W riting about a controversial topic and trying to come up with new concepts and ideas proved to be a formidable task. My book greatly benefited from the knowledge and assistance generously provided by the following people.

Thanks must go to Kyle Sarofeen, co-founder and publisher of Hamilcar Publications, for his unwavering support, enthusiasm, advice, and guidance. I also owe a debt of gratitude to Tris Dixon, author of *Damage: The Untold Story of Brain Trauma in Boxing*. His book chronicled the lives of fighters suffering from boxing-induced brain damage. Reading *Damage* inspired me to write a book that offered solutions to professional boxing's biggest problems. I consider our books, both published by Hamilcar, a kind of literary "one-two punch." I believe that together these books can effect positive change.

Deserving of special mention are Bobby Franklin, publisher of Boxing OverBroadway.com, and Dan Cuoco, director of the International Boxing Research Organization and editor of its quarterly journal. Both generously gave their time and expertise to critique excerpts from the manuscript and offer valuable insights and suggestions.

This book, by necessity, had to rely on the accurate records of hundreds of individual prizefighters. For providing a treasure trove of valuable data and information I am deeply indebted to BoxRec.com and The Manuel Velazquez Boxing Fatality Collection. BoxRec.com, founded in 2000, is the official recordkeeper for combat sports worldwide and an indispensable resource for authors, historians, and fans. Manuel Velazquez was an anti-boxing activist who began assembling his vast collection in the mid-20th century. Joseph R. Svinth, the current curator, acquired the collection in 1998, and for the past quarter century, he has been responsible for adding to, correcting, and digitizing this remarkable collection. It now includes information on 2,077 boxing fatalities—both professional and amateur—that occurred from 1724 to 2019.

I also wish to thank Erik Arnold, the son of former professional boxer Tony Arnold, for taking the time to discuss and analyze the problems facing the sport and for critiquing several chapters. I am also grateful to Ted Lidsky, neuroscientist and former amateur boxer. In addition to his boxing expertise and computer skills, Ted helped me to better understand the complexities of brain trauma and concussion.

I also want to commend the artistic skill of Brad Norr, creative director for Hamilcar, who designed the striking cover of the book using a photograph I had taken decades earlier.

The help and support I received from Iris Topel was invaluable. Her sharp eye for detail helped to make a good manuscript even better.

My gratitude extends to Tony Gee, who shared his extraordinary knowledge of the pre-Queensberry era of bare-knuckle boxing.

I am also grateful for having benefited over the years from the research, analyses, and writings of boxing historians Chuck Hasson, Mike Casey, Mike Hunnicut, and Springs Toledo. Thanks to Teddy Atlas, Steve Farhood, Lou DiBella, and J. Russell Peltz for sharing their sharp observations and keen insight. Thanks also to Joshua Meng and Terry Matzner, two boxing mavens whose correspondence was both enlightening and entertaining.

There are many other people to thank who, in various ways, made a difficult task somewhat easier by offering information, encouragement, and feedback: Russ Anber, Steve Canton, Matt Farrago, Bonny Fetterman, Melissa Gerstein, Elizabeth Gittman, Phil Guarneri, Austin Killeen, Morrie Krasnitz, Mitch Levin, Don Majeski, Adam Pollack, Ron Scott Stevens, Sean Sullivan, Harold Weston, Mike Wolf, Steve Zellman, and Greg Zola. If I have inadvertently overlooked anyone in these acknowledgments, please accept my sincere apologies.

Finally, I am profoundly grateful to my brother Bennett and my sister-in-law Gail, who so generously gave of their time to review chapters while offering valuable feedback, support, and helpful suggestions for this book. I feel blessed to have you both in my corner.

Bibliography

Anderson, Jack. *The Legality of Boxing: A Punch Drunk Love?* London and New York: Routledge, 2009.

Brady, Jim. *Boxing Confidential: Power, Corruption and the Richest Prize in Sport.* Lytham, Lancashire, UK: Milo, 2002.

Callis, Tracy, Chuck Hasson, and Mike DeLisa. *Philadelphia's Boxing Heritage: 1876–1976.* Charleston, SC: Arcadia, 2002.

Callis, Tracy, and Chuck Johnston. *Boxing in the Los Angeles Area: 1880–2005.* Victoria, BC: Trafford, 2009.

Cannon, Jimmy. *Nobody Asked Me, But . . . The World of Jimmy Cannon.* Edited by Jack Cannon and Tom Cannon. New York: Holt, Rinehart and Winston, 1978.

Dixon, Tris. *Damage: The Untold Story of Brain Trauma in Boxing.* Boston: Hamilcar, 2021.

———. *The Road to Nowhere: A Journey through Boxing's Wastelands.* Durrington, UK: Pitch, 2014.

Early, Gerald, ed. *The Cambridge Companion to Boxing.* Cambridge, UK: Cambridge University Press, 2019.

Eig, Jonathan. *Ali: A Life.* Boston and New York: Houghton Mifflin Harcourt, 2017.

Fitch, Jerry. *Cleveland Arena: Ohio's Professional Boxing Mecca, 1937–1973.* Charleston, SC: Arcadia, 2022.

Fleischer, Nat. *50 Years at Ringside.* New York: Fleet, 1958.

Fried, Ronald K. *Corner Men, Great Boxing Trainers*. New York: Four Walls Eight Windows, 1991.

Gee, Tony. *Up to Scratch: Bareknuckle Fighting and Heroes of the Prize-ring*. Herts, UK: Queen Anne, 1998.

Goldman, Herbert G. *Boxing: A Worldwide Record of Bouts and Boxers*, vols. 3 and 4. Jefferson, NC: McFarland, 2012.

Goldstein, Ruby, as told to Frank Graham. *Third Man in the Ring*. New York: Funk & Wagnalls, 1959.

Gorn, Elliott J. *The Manly Art: Bare-Knuckle Prize Fighting in America*. Ithaca and London: Cornell University, 1986.

Haislett, Edwin. *Boxing*. New York: A.S. Barnes, 1940.

Hasson, Chuck. *Philadelphia's Boxing History Scrapbook 1843 to 2020*. Self-Published, 2021.

Hodgson, Voigt R., and L. Murray Thomas. *Boxing Gloves Compared Using Dummy Head Acceleration Response*. Detroit: Department of Neurosurgery, Wayne State University, 1981.

Hugman, Barry J., and Sean Willis, ed. *The Definitive History of World Championship Boxing*. United Kingdom: G2 Entertainment, 2016.

Interim Report and Recommendations of the State of New Jersey Commission of Investigation on the Inadequate Regulation of Boxing. March 1, 1984.

Laskas, Jeanne Marie. *Concussion*. New York: Random House, 2015.

Margolick, David. *Beyond Glory: Joe Louis vs. Max Schmeling, and a World on the Brink*. New York: Alfred A. Knopf, 2005.

Mercante, Arthur, with Phil Guarnieri. *Inside the Ropes*. Ithaca, NY: McBooks, 2006.

Mitchell, Kevin. *Jacobs Beach: The Mob, the Fights, the Fifties*. New York: Pegasus, 2010.

Nagler, Barney. *James Norris and the Decline of Boxing*. New York: Bobbs-Merrill, 1964.

Neidecker, John, and Joshua Martin. "Mortality Resulting from Head Injury in Professional Boxing Revisited: Fatalities from 2000–2019." *Journal of Combat Sports Medicine*. Supplement to volume 4, number 1, January 2022, pp. 38–44.

Nevada State Athletic Commission. *Ringside and Training Principles*. 2001.

Newfield, Jack. *Only in America: The Life and Crimes of Don King*. New York: William Morrow, 1995.

Oates, Joyce Carol. *On Boxing*. Garden City, NY: Dolphin/Doubleday, 1987.

Organized Crime in Boxing: Final Boxing Report of the State of New Jersey Commission of Investigations. December 16, 1985.

Phimster, Ian, and David Patrick, eds. *Ted Carroll: A Boxing Legacy*. Lanham, MD: Rowman & Littlefield, 2023.

Professional Boxing in Quebec: A Study (English version). Regie de la securite dans les sports, 1981.

Report of the Joint Legislative Committee on Professional Boxing. State of New York, March 15, 1963.

Rodriguez, Robert G. *The Regulation of Boxing: A History and Comparative Analysis of Policies among American States*. Jefferson, NC: McFarland, 2009.

Sammons, Jeffrey T. *Beyond the Ring: The Role of Boxing in American Society*. Urbana: University of Illinois Press, 1988.

Schulberg, Budd. *Ringside: A Treasury of Boxing Reportage*. Chicago: Ivan R. Dee. 2006.

Silver, Mike. *The Arc of Boxing: The Rise and Decline of the Sweet Science*. Jefferson, NC: McFarland, 2008.

———. *The Night the Referee Hit Back: Memorable Moments from the World of Boxing*. Lanham, MD: Rowman & Littlefield, 2020.

———. *Stars in the Ring: Jewish Champions in the Golden Age of Boxing*. Guilford, CT: Lyons, 2016.

Southern California Advisory Committee on Boxing Safeguards. California State Athletic Commission, 1964.

Summerskill, Edith. *The Ignoble Art*. London: Heinemann, 1956.

Svinth, Joseph, R. "Death Under the Spotlight: The Manuel Velazquez Boxing Fatality Collection," *Journal of Combative Sports,* October 2011.

Toledo, Springs. *The Gods of War*. Tora Book, 2014.

Weston, Stanley. *The Best of the Ring*. Chicago: Bonus, 1992.

———, and Steve Farhood. *Boxing: The 20th Century*. New York: BDD Promotional, 1993.

Periodicals

Boxing and Wrestling
Boxing Illustrated/Wrestling News
Boxing Monthly
Esquire

International Boxing Research Organization
Journal of Combat Sports Medicine
Las Vegas Review-Journal
New York Post
New York Times
Philadelphia Inquirer
The Ring
Sports Illustrated
Tonight's Boxing Program
Wall Street Journal

Interviews
Russ Anber, January 5, 2025
Lou DiBella, October 16, 2023
Ted Lidsky, July 16, 2024
J Russell Peltz, July 28, 2023

Notes

Introduction

[1] Joseph R. Svinth. "Death Under the Spotlight: The Manuel Velazquez Boxing Fatality Collection," *Journal of Combative Sports*, October 2011. https://ejmas.com/jcs/velazquez/.

[2] "Boxers Who Died in 2022," EssentiallySports.com.

[3] The fight the author refers to: Subriel Matias vs. Maxim Dadashev (see chapter 2).

[4] The abbreviations stand for Word Boxing Council, World Boxing Association, International Boxing Federation, and World Boxing Organization.

[5] John Neidecker and Joshua Martin. "Mortality Resulting from Head Injury in Professional Boxing Revisited: Fatalities from 2000–2019." *Journal of Combat Sports Medicine*, Supplement to vol. 4, no. 1, January 2022, p. 38.

[6] Rod Serling. *Requiem for a Heavyweight: A Reading Version of the Dramatic Script* (New York: Bantam, 1962), p. vii.

Chapter 1

[7] Tony Gee. *Up to Scratch*: *Bareknuckle Fighting and Heroes of the Prize-ring* (London: Queen Anne, 2001), p. 15.

[8] Tony Gee. "Fresh Light on the 'New Rules' of 1838," *International Boxing Research Organization* (December 2021), pp. 14–15.

[9] Tony Gee. "The Demise of the (Bareknuckle) Traditional Prize-ring in Britain: A Brief Look at Some Pertinent Causes," *The British Boxing Board*

of Control Boxing Yearbook 2009, ed. by Barry J. Hugman (Edinburgh and London: Mainstream, 2008), p. 47.

[10]Elliott J. Gorn, *The Manly Art: Bare-Knuckle Prize Fighting in America* (Ithaca and London: Cornell University Press, 1986), pp. 204, 205.

[11]Ian Harvey. "The Longest Boxing Match in History Went 110 Rounds and Lasted 7 Hours," *The Vintage News,* March 6, 2019.

[12]Jeffrey T. Sammons. *Beyond the Ring: The Rise of Boxing in American Society* (Urbana: University of Illinois Press, 1988), p. 149.

[13]Nick Parkinson. "Mayweather–Pacquiao—Revisiting the Richest Fight in Boxing History." ESPN.com. May 2, 2020.

[14]"Paul vs. Diaz Does Over 500,000 PPV Buys." Fightsports.tv.com. August 18, 2023.

Chapter 2

[15]Ben Morse. "Each Year, 13 Boxers on Average Die in the Ring." CNN.com. October 17, 2019.

[16]Chris Pleasance and James Dutton. "The Punches That Killed Maxim Dadeshev." DailyMail.com. July 24, 2019.

[17]Ibid.

[18]John Neidecker and Joshua Martin. "Mortality Resulting from Head Injury in Professional Boxing Revisited: Fatalities from 2000–2019." *Journal of Combat Sports Medicine*, Supplement to vol. 4, no. 1, January 2022, p. 39.

[19]Ibid., pp. 40–41.

[20]Ibid., p. 41.

[21]Ibid., p. 42.

[22]Svinth, Manuel Velazquez Boxing Fatality Collection, 1980–1999.

[23]Bobby Franklin, "Murder in Montreal." BoxingOverBroadway.com. December 2018.

[24]Neidecker and Martin, "Mortality," p. 40.

Chapter 3

[25]Stanley Weston and Steven Farhood. *The Ring: Boxing in the 20th Century* (New York: BDD Illustrated, 1993), pp. 54–65.

[26]Tracy Callis, Chuck Hasson, and Mike De Lisa. *Philadelphia's Boxing Heritage, 1876–1976* (Charleston, SC: Arcadia, 2002), p. 9.

[27]Email correspondence with Chuck Hasson, July 24, 2024.

[28]Callis et al., *Philadelphia's Boxing*, p. 25.

[29]Svinth, Manuel Velazquez Boxing Fatality Collection, in California, 1921–1941.

[30]https://en.wikipedia.org/wiki/1914_California_Proposition_20.

[31]Tracy Callis and Chuck Johnston. *Boxing in the Los Angeles Area, 1880–2005* (Victoria, Canada: Trafford, 2009), p. 37.

[32]Ibid., pp. 38, 39.

[33]Svinth, Manuel Velazquez Boxing Fatality Collection, in California, 1914–1935.

[34]"History of New York Boxing Legislation, Rules & Regulation." BoxRec.com.

[35]Howard M. Tuckner. "End of a Boxing Era: It Was Zany, It Was Noisy, It Was St. Nick's," *New York Times*, May 13, 1962, p. 57.

[36]Svinth, Manuel Velazquez Boxing Fatality Collection, in New York, 1906–1949.

[37]Ibid., 1950–1961.

Chapter 4

[38]"Boxing Referee Salary." www.comparably.com.

Chapter 5

[39]Robert H. Boyle. "No Man Was His Keeper," *Sports Illustrated,* March 24, 1980. https://vault.si.com/vault/1980/03/24.

[40]Ibid.

[41]Ibid.

[42]Bennett Derby, M.D. Transcription of concussion video, 1982.

Chapter 6

[43]Andrew Carlton and Robin Marc Orr. "The Effects of Fluid Loss on Physical Performance: A Critical Review," *Journal of Sport and Science*, vol. 4, no. 4, December 2015, pp. 357–363.

[44]Paul McReath. "It's Time to Re-Examine the Weigh-In Day," *East Sider Boxing Archives*, January 30, 2007.

[45]Wallace Matthews. "Fight Doc Warns About Risk of Weigh-Ins." NewYorkPost.com. April 16, 2000.

[46]Jason Burgos. "UFC Deaths: Taking a Look into the Dark Side of Cage Fighting." Sportsnaut.com. Updated February 19, 2024.

Chapter 8

[47]Mike Silver. *The Arc of Boxing: The Rise and Decline of the Sweet Science,* (Jefferson, NC: McFarland, 2008), p. 51.

[48]Ibid., p. 52

[49]In determining today's average (as of 2024) I only considered champions recognized by the WBC, WBA, WBO, and IBF in the eight traditional weight divisions.

[50]Silver, *The Arc of Boxing*, pp. 55–56.

[51]Stanley Weston and Steven Farhood. *The Ring: Boxing in the 20th Century.* (New York: BDD Illustrated, 1993), pp. 63, 136, 148, 160, 183, 254.

[52]World title fights in 2022. BoxRec.com.

[53]BoxRec.com.

[54]Silver, *The Arc of Boxing,* pp. 57–58.

[55]Ibid., p. 64.

[56]*Boxing: The Naval Aviation Physical Training Manual* (Aviation Training Division: Office of the Chief of Naval Operations:1943), pp. 105–110.

Chapter 9

[57]Dave Brady. "Ali Crowing after Results of Mayo Tests." WashingtonPost.com. July 25, 1980.

[58]Tris Dixon. *Damage: The Untold Story of Brain Trauma in Boxing* (Boston: Hamilcar, 2021), p. 152.

[59]Ibid., p. 149.

[60]Ibid., p. 152.

[61]Ibid., p. 150.

[62]Ibid., p. 155.

[63]Ibid.

Chapter 12

[64]Svinth, Manuel Velazquez Boxing Fatality Collection.

[65]Ibid. Table 13.

[66]BoxRec.com. Additional information was provided by email communication with Joseph R. Svinth, August 22 and 28, 2022.

[67]Roman Stubbs. "The Olympics Banned Headgear for Male Boxers, but Not Women." washingtonpost.com. August 8, 2015.

68Ken Belsen. "Making Olympic Boxing Safer by Eliminating Head Guards." nytimes.com. August 6, 2016.
69"Stoking a Debate on Safety and Sexism." WashingtonPost.com. August 15, 2016.
70Ryan Richelsen. "Will Removing Headgear Make Boxing Safer?" nd.edu/biomechanics. March 6, 2019.
71J. Walilki, D. C. Viano, and C. A. Bir. "Biomechanics of the Head for Olympic Boxer Punches to the Face," *British Journal of Sports Medicine*, vol. 39, no. 10. October 2005.
72Tris Dixon. *Damage: The Untold Story of Brain Trauma in Boxing* (Boston: Hamilcar, 2021), p. 116.
73Anne Tjonndal et al. 2022. "Concussions, Cuts and Cracked Bones: A Systematic Literature Review on Protective Headgear and Head Injury Prevention in Olympic Boxing." National Library of Medicine. nih.gov.
74Steven P. Broglio et al. "The Efficacy of Soccer Headgear," *Journal of Athletic Training*, July-September 2003, pp. 220-224.

Chapter 13
75Joe Ward, Josh Williams, and Sam Manchester. "N.F.L. Brains." nytimes.com. July 25, 2017.
76Lisa Brown. "CTE Risk More than Doubles after Just Three Years of Playing Football," *The Brink*, bu.edu. October 7, 2019.
77"Researchers Find CTE in 345 of 376 Former NFL Players." bu.edu. February 6, 2023.
78Paul Stone. "Boxers and Brain Injuries–A Scary Study." Neurologic Rehabilitation Institute at Brookhaven Hospital (NRI), January 14, 2023.
79American Association of Neurological Surgeons. aans.org. April 11, 2024.
80"110 N.F.L. Brains," Boston University Research-CTE Center. bu.edu.
81Sam Borden, Mike Grondahl, and Joe Ward. "What Happened Within This Player's Skull." nytimes.com. January 9, 2017.
82Wikipedia. Mike Webster.
83David Webner and Grant L. Iverson. "Suicide in Professional American Football in the Past 95 Years." researchgate.net. October 2016.
84Jonathan Abrams. "Phillip Adams Had Severe C.T.E. at the Time of Shootings." nytimes.com. December 16, 2021.
85Wikipedia. Jovan Belcher.

[86]"NFL Modifies Concussion Protocol after Review of Tagovailoa Injury." pbs.org/newshour. October 9, 2022.
[87]Interview with Ted Lidsky, July 16, 2024.
[88]Jonathan Eig, *Ali: A Life* (New York: Houghton, Mifflin Harcourt, 2017), pp. 299 and 545.

Chapter 14
[89]Justin Block. "Despite All the Blood, MMA Is Actually Safer than Boxing." Huffpost.com. December 29, 2016.
[90]Charles Bernick et al. "Repeated Head Trauma Is Associated with Smaller Thalamic Volumes and Slower Processing Speed: The Professional Fighter's Brain Health Study," *British Journal of Sports Medicine.* bjsm.bmj.com.
[91]Ross Canning. "How Many Fighters Have Died in the Ring: Boxing and MMA." Mmamicks.com. September 10, 2019
[92]Svinth, Manuel Velazquez Boxing Fatality Collection.

Chapter 15
[93]Red Smith, "Jim Cagney Takes Off the Gloves," *New York Times*, September 11, 1974, p. 51.
[94]Email correspondence with Tony Gee, August 8, 2021.
[95]E. Magraken, "Study—Updated Bare Knuckle Boxing Injury Data." CombatSportsLaw.com, August 16, 2021.
[96]State of New York, *Report of the Joint Legislative Committee on Professional Boxing,* March 15, 1963, p. 170.
[97]Interview with Russ Anber, January 5, 2025.
[98]State of New York, *Report of the Joint Legislative Committee,* pp. 169 and 185a.
[99]*Southern California Advisory Committee on Boxing Safeguards.* Equipment Safety Procedures Committee, 1964, p. 1 (section 2).
[100]Voigt R. Hodgson and L. Murray Thomas. "Boxing Gloves Compared Using Dummy Head Acceleration Response," Department. of Neurology, Wayne State University, November 17, 1981, p. 8.
[101]Ibid., p. 9.
[102]Ibid., p. 11.
[103]Ibid., p. 12.
[104]Jeff Tracy. "Study: Cumulative Force of Impacts—Not Concussion—Predicts CTE." Axios.com. June 22, 2023.

Chapter 16

[105]Pete Hamill. "Blood on Their Hands," *Esquire*, June 1996, p. 94.
[106]World Boxing Council, World Boxing Association, International Boxing Federation, World Boxing Organization.
[107]Jack Newfield. "The Shame of Boxing," *The Nation,* November 12, 2001, p. 14.
[108]Ibid., p. 18.
[109]Sean Nam. "Court, Public Docs Show Third Party 'Lobbyist' Receiving Payments for Rankings Connected to WBA." BoxingScene.com. July 17, 2022.
[110]Matt Christie. "Editor's Letter: The Actions of Sanctioning Bodies Leave Errol Spence Perplexed and Me Wanting to Bang My Head against a Brick Wall." BoxingNews.com. June 22, 2023.
[111]Interview with J. Russell Peltz, July 28, 2023.
[112]Stanley Weston and Steven Farhood. *The Ring: Boxing in the 20th Century* (New York: BDD Illustrated, 1993), pp. 36–191.
[113]Svinth, Manuel Velazquez Boxing Fatality Collection.
[114]Ronald Smothers. "IBF Supervision Ends; Founder Gets 22 Months." NYTimes.com. February 15, 2001.
[115]Jim Brady. *Boxing Confidential: Power, Corruption, and the Richest Prize in Sport* (Lytham, Lancashire, U.K.: Milo, 2002), p. 165.
[116]Springs Toledo. *The Gods of War* (Tora Book, 2014), p. 77.
[117]Statistic provided by Chris Smith of the International Boxing Research Organization.
[118]Wallace Matthews. "King's in the Hall—Only in America," *New York Post*, January 15, 1997, p. 67.
[119]Brady, *Boxing Confidential*, p. 263.
[120]Ibid., p. 258.
[121]Ibid.

Chapter 17
[122]Svinth, Manuel Velazquez Boxing Fatality Collection.

Chapter 18
[123]Interview with Lou DiBella, October 16, 2023.

Index

About the Author

Mike Silver is an internationally respected boxing historian and author. His work has appeared in *The New York Times*, *The Ring* magazine, *Boxing Monthly*, *International Boxing Research Organization Journal*, and various boxing websites. A former inspector for the New York State Athletic Commission, he has served as a consultant and on-air commentator for nineteen boxing documentaries produced by PBS, HBO, ESPN, the History Channel, and Madison Square Garden Network. Mike is the author of three previous books, including *The Arc of Boxing: The Rise and Decline of the Sweet Science*, one of the most accurate, fact-based analyses of boxing and boxers ever written.

When in Doubt, Stop the Bout is set in 10-point Sabon, which was designed by the Germanborn typographer and designer Jan Tschichold (1902–1974) in the period 1964–1967. It was released jointly by the Linotype, Monotype, and Stempel type foundries in 1967. Copyeditor for this project was Boutros Salah. The book was designed by Brad Norr Design, Minneapolis, Minnesota, and typeset by Westchester Publishing Services. Printed and manufactured by Lightning Source on acid-free paper.

9 781949 590777